The Way Things work in life ©

Dr. Basimah Khulusi M.D.
Edited by Olivia

To my daughter Camellia
For she gave me life

Cover picture: Asymmetric polyhedra created using the "patent pending" method
invented by Dr. Basimah Khulusi M.D.: Apparatus And Method For Modeling All
Matter By Modeling, Truncating, And Creating N-Dimensional Polyhedra Including
Those Having Holes, Concave Attributes, And No Symmetry.
(Representing geometric structures of different families)

TABLE OF CONTENTS

INTRODUCTION

All throughout my life, I've been watching bad things happen to people around me, and to myself, and asking why? Not knowing why things happen the way they do was more agonizing than the bad events themselves, because it didn't make sense to me how life could be so unfair!

I found myself asking, "Why?" I saw other people asking, "Why?" As if knowing why would have made a difference. Because after something has happened already, knowing why would not change a thing. But if everybody needs that knowledge, it means it is important. Maybe it makes things easier to bear. That knowledge also might make us wiser so next time we can choose better, and maybe control the outcome and make things work better in our favor. So it might be that knowing why would actually make a difference in our future.

Why do I think I can explain things?

Being a physician and an inventor, and having been exposed to multiple different cultures from around the world, I couldn't help but notice that there are patterns of human behavior, and that therefore, there are mechanisms of action underlying events and happenings. I had to uncover these mechanisms because understanding them would explain to me why this world sometimes seems to be so unjust. For example, I needed to understand why bad things happen to good people, and how come it seems that bad people don't get punished for their deeds. Understanding certainly would not make the hurt any easier and might not help the heart very much, but it will help the brain. I've been trying to figure out the answers to these questions all my life.

If my trying to answer these questions sounds pretentious, it might be because I have set out to accomplish a very ambitious task. I am asking you to become the judge, and decide whether you like my answers or not. You do not have to buy what I am telling you. If my arguments make sense to you, so be it. If not, then all I want to do is to stir intelligent debate, because that will be the best way to bring out the various aspects of the subject. Please prove me wrong. Only intelligent debate is allowed, and no hitting below the belt, please.

So why does life seem to be so unfair? Or is it? I just needed to understand.

Why do things work that way? Is there a God? And if there is a God, how come God can be so unjust?

I found the answer in mathematics, chemistry and physics, and I found that mathematics and chemistry and physics and all the laws and everything that we know are "God." God is everything. When I finally found the answer, it all came together for me, and I felt reassured and relieved. And now, I want you to know, because what you're about to find out is that in the long run, everything will be OK.

THE WORD GOD IS A METAPHOR

People have tried to answer these questions about life in the past. They used the metaphors of their day and age, as well as of their professions, the way religious people and philosophers did. Old metaphors might have resonated with people back then and might still make sense to some today, but that is leaving out a multitude of others who are finding it difficult to relate to this language; especially the young.

First, let me tell you why I am using the word "metaphor" to refer to the words used. A metaphor is defined in the English dictionary as "something used, or regarded as being used, to represent something else; emblem; symbol." If we thoroughly think about it, that definition applies to all of the words we use to name everything that we know, and I'll elaborate on that later.

People nowadays have become disenchanted by old teachings that have used old metaphors from the remote past. There is dissonance between those metaphors and the knowledge they have been acquiring during their lifetime from school. When school teaches them that everything has a scientific explanation, and then the teachings about life's issues tell them to believe things that have no scientific basis, their minds get confused (to say the least) and they refuse to just believe. When science tells us that believing in ideas that have no proof are "delusions" that indicate a diseased mind, and then religion asks us to believe there is a God with personal characteristics, and heaven and hell and other "delusions" that have no proof, our mind cannot help but struggle with those inconsistencies.

In this book, my answers will be given using the language and understandings that people have been acquiring in school.

How does using new metaphor make things different for us from the way old metaphors have always explained things for human beings? In the past, and still up to this day, whenever we couldn't explain what causes something to happen, we would say it is "God"–like in the example of a tsunami. Science now can explain how an earthquake deep in the ocean somewhere could generate it. But before that happened, it was an act of God. So just like the tsunami has a scientific explanation, everything else in life has a scientific explanation also. Until we figure out what it is, we say that the reason for what happened is God, and if what happened is a bad thing, we say God is punishing us. But once we understand the mechanism of action, then we say it is science.

So what does that mean exactly? It means what used to be God causing an event that we didn't understand becomes science when we are able to understand it. That means the difference between God and science is our understanding, our "thoughts." Therefore, is "God" equal to "science?" That begs the next question: Where did the laws of science come from? We certainly did not make them. It was not us who decided that a special earthquake could generate forces that would lift and propel a wall of water above it and create a tsunami. That phenomenon follows the laws of physics. We observe these laws, we decipher them using our brain, and we use them to our advantage whenever we can—but we do not make them. These laws exist by themselves. Similarly, we explain all other phenomena that we understand using scientific laws. Does that make them not God anymore? Why not? It's just a matter of semantics. So if we used to call these laws "God" before we understood them, we could still call them "God" after we understand them, which makes "God" all of these laws. God is the LAW. God is "everything."

GOD IS EVERYTHING

God is everything including us: we are part of God because we are part of everything. We exist and the laws exist and we are all part of the whole, which is God. We understand the laws of science using our brain, but we did not make our brain either. We can say God gave it to us, but that is good only until we figure out the scientific mechanism that generates it, and then we will say it is science and these are the laws of how that happened. At that time we forget that we did not make any of these laws, and that we just translated them; these laws existed and operated before we were able to explain them. Where did these laws come from? Well, they just exist. These laws are God, science is God and everything is God—God is everything.

God is the air and the earth and the fire and the water and the elements and the forces and the animals and the plants and the thoughts and the spirits and the essence. God is not sitting up there somewhere in a chair with a clipboard and a pen in his hand monitoring things and modifying and adjusting them as needed. No, God is not limited like that. God is the "Law" that sets the laws of the forces—then the forces set the structures and the mechanisms in motion.

So what is the "Law?" I won't profess to know what the "Law" is. Physicists are currently looking for it. It might be one force that generates all the different forces depending on the proportions and concentrations involved. Nobody knows yet. But we can understand a lot of the forces generated by it, and the structures formed by these forces, and how the machine works. Nobody can refuse to acknowledge the presence of the "Law," but some people refuse to acknowledge the presence of a God. They can call the "Law" whatever they want. I will call it God in English.

French people refer to God as "Dieu," Arabs refer to God as "Allah" or "Elah" or "Rabb," and Jews refer to God as "El" or "Elah" or "Yahweh." Moslems also refer to God as "Allahumma." and Jews as "Elohim" (a coincidence?). But does that mean that God and Dieu and Allah and Yahweh are not the same? Of course they are because they are everything, and everything is one thing. For those who believe there is only one God, you must believe that God created all people and all languages, then you must believe that those people who have a different language can use a different word to refer to that one God. Therefore, everybody is talking about the same thing. So let's not get lost in the semantics and pay attention to what's real. For the purpose of this book that I am writing in English, I will call everything God.

But using a word is limiting to the vastness of what God is. That's why Judaism refers to God by a symbol that should not even be pronounced (YHWH). Other people read the symbol as Yahweh, but shouldn't. Some people refer to God as he or she or whatever. Using metaphor this way makes it easier on humans to talk about God, and figure out an accessible concept for the idea of God.

That's why depicting God as a human being has been very successful in serving that purpose for thousands of years for many different cultures all over the world starting, as far as we know it, with the ancient Egyptians' God Horus. Then there is Hindus' Krishna and Christianity's Christ (a coincidence?) and other civilizations' gods until this day. But other cultures have refused to even pronounce a word for God, or depict God in a human form, like in Judaism and Islam. The Jewish religion has names of God that describe God's attributes, same as in the Islamic religion (a coincidence?). That makes it easier for the mind to grasp the idea of what God is, and how all-encompassing God is because God is everything.

Human beings are part of God: we human beings did not create our brains or ourselves. We are part of God, a part of everything. Whenever one of us has a baby, we cannot help but marvel at it being a "miracle." Is there a human being that does not acknowledge that fact? So if a baby is a "miracle" then what does that make us? It makes us "big miracles." That's exactly what we are. Being alive and having the brain that we have allows us to be able to decipher the laws operating around us, and harness the forces to create things that serve our purpose. In the process of doing that, we end up feeling so powerful and almighty and we forget that we have just used the tools that have already been given to us, including a capable brain. We have simply put things together, and that makes us feel very good because that process is usually not easy.

We are like the spider that can use the brain it was given to build an intricate web, engineered with the correct angles and geometric shapes that will make it withstand strong blows of wind without breaking. Or, like the bees that can build a stratified community good for the survival of many generations of bees. Or like the monarch butterflies that can navigate thousands of miles of the sky to get to their destination, etc.

We use the tools we are given to accomplish great things, and they use the tools they are given to accomplish great things also.

We are part of the "everything," and everything is a miracle.

GOD IS FAIR

God is the law, and everything is generated from this law including all the laws that govern everything. It all unfolds following these laws, and it works the way we observe it to work by itself. When we figure out the mechanism of action of these laws and all the checks and balances built in them, we realize how smart they are because they take care of business automatically, and everything will be OK in the end. Everything will work out for the best on the big scale of things.

I'll give you a very quick simplified example here: how many times have we heard the story about rich peoples' kids who are given everything or feel entitled to be given everything and how they end up lacking the oomph and endurance to achieve success (and/or they become destructive)? Generation upon generation, they lose the money that the hard-working parents made. Either that happens, or the parents (fearing that will happen) deprive their children from their hard earned money so that they won't waste it, because they did not work hard to get it. So the parents end up locking the money in a very secure trust fund that is not controlled by the children, or they give it to charities, or sometimes even to caregivers of their dogs, etc. That leads to redistribution of their wealth. Two contemporary examples are Bill Gates and Warren Buffet who spent all of their lives accumulating billions of dollars, but they will not leave their billions to their descendants! Most of their hard earned money will go to charities. That makes life more fair on the larger scale.

This example—which operates at the family level—operates also at larger levels. For example, some citizens of rich nations who get a sense of entitlement will end up lacking the oomph and endurance to achieve big things as well.

On the other hand, somebody who is poor and/or lacking and wanting will have all the oomph and endurance needed to struggle very hard and withstand pain and suffering until they become rich ... Then they become rich and their kids become spoiled and so on and so forth. The wheel turns and what goes up comes back down and life stays fair. If it wasn't for that law, then the rich and their kids would keep their riches forever, and the poor would stay poor forever, end of story! Life wouldn't be fair. But it doesn't happen that way; life takes care of itself because of the laws that have been set, because of science.

And, "What are the laws that operated in this instance," you might ask? The law that says, "What goes up must come down": that everything cycles. Then you ask, "What was the mechanism of action of that law?" It works following the laws of cause and effect. I'll give you a very simplified example to make it clear. First, let's set it up like a mathematical equation to consider the variables we need to study. The first variable will be that the parents are rich. The next variable is that the kids end up having a sense of entitlement, not much ambition, and no sense of urgency to achieve much, because they don't know what to strive for. The reason is that they already have the rewards all around them and they notice it does not give them much happiness. As I clarify later, happiness is in getting rewarded for what YOU ACHIEVE. Therefore happiness is in the sacrificing and heartache and struggle on the way towards achieving great things, and the efforts put into getting your ambitions fulfilled; but once you're there, then what? Well for these kids, they are already there—they already have "the carrot at the end of the stick," and their perspective on life is different. The third variable is that they end up lacking enough ambition and endurance and oomph to achieve much. Then you get the outcome of that equation, which is that the parents' money often does not end up with their kids nor does it stay with their kids. Again that is the most simplified way of explaining what happens.

Now, I am sure some people are going to scream, "Not true!" and then proceed to give me examples about how what I have just said does not apply in this or that instance. I know that the outcome described above does not happen immediately in every instance of rich people's kids whom you can observe during a certain set period of time, and in one generation. But there is a scientific explanation for that also. The explanation is that the mathematical equation could have other variables in it that change the outcome. One variable that would change the outcome is when the descendants are not given any sense of entitlement from very early on, but they are given a sense of duty instead, and they have to work hard and suffer and sacrifice like everybody else. That's what is being done with Prince

William and Prince Harry, for example. They have to go to school, they have to join the service, hold a regular job, and even go to war if need be … That is what ends up changing the equation. So the riches are kept for a while in a very structured setting, where the descendants don't have a free reign over it either. Everybody knows that if kids are spoiled, they become "spoiled rotten," i.e. "no good!" Therefore, there are instances where the outcome of losing the riches is delayed, and that is when duty, structure, hard work and sacrifice are added to the equation. But it cannot be avoided forever. Just look at the multitude of examples around you and in history.

Of course there are other forces that cause redistribution of the wealth of the rich, but in the example above, I was just focusing on the family dynamics part.

Another example that shows how the laws have been set to make life fair is the example of food. I am sure many of you are aware now of what the healthiest diet should be, and it goes this way in order of importance: no overeating, whole grains, legumes, seeds, vegetables, fruit, dairy, and a little meat—and not necessarily including all these food items listed. Whose diet is that if not poor people's diet? And I don't mean by that the poor people of America who eat hamburgers and other unhealthy foods. No, I mean the real brunt of poor people of the world because the list above is that of the cheapest way to eat. So as you can see, the poor people's diet is the healthiest, and the rich people's food that is abundant, processed, and rich in animal protein and fat is not healthy and causes disease! Do you see now how things in life are kept fair?

Rich people have benefits and problems in their lives inherent to the fact that they are rich, and of course, poor people have benefits and problems in their lives inherent to the fact that they are poor. Which life would be better, you might ask? Permit me to answer you with a question: If poor people's lives were so miserable because they are poor, how come they don't all end up in a depression, or how come we don't see them all committing suicide? Also, how come some rich people get depressed, sabotage their lives and kill themselves?

We also see that principal of fairness operating at scales larger than the individual. What goes up must come down. Big companies fail, and smaller companies grow. Empires fall and new ones develop. Big systems collapse and others emerge.

EVERY SYSTEM HAS IN IT THE SEEDS OF ITS OWN DEMISE. This ensures that there will always be a chance for the little guy.

In our economic system, when companies trade their shares publicly, they need to show increased revenue and income for their stock price to go up. If their revenue and income stay the same or decrease, their stock price declines. Therefore, these companies are under pressure to grow their revenues and incomes, and are forced to resort to different tactics to do that. Knowing that greed and shortsightedness are often a part of the equation, some companies resort to doing things that have bad outcomes for them on the large scale and in the more distant future. For example, they outsource the production of their products overseas for cheaper labor to improve their balance sheets, thus causing a decrease in the jobs in their country, which results in less purchasing power of consumers in their country, which will result in a decrease of their revenue. Another thing that companies do is cut corners to show decreased expenses. For example, some goods production companies and airline companies cut back on the number of their employees and ask them to do more work to increase their productivity. That leads to increased emotional and physical strain, which results in more absenteeism, injuries, worker's compensation expenses, air traffic accidents, and decreased revenue and increased expenses. Another thing they do is cut expenses on essential things like safety. The best example is what happened in the BP oil well blowup in the Gulf of Mexico. Everyone can only imagine how large the cost of that disaster will end up being. Similarly, some banks have been filling their pockets at the expense of the economic survival of their customers. Some pharmaceutical companies and medical companies have been resorting to conducting non-kosher business also for the sake of their stock price. They have been manufacturing markets for their drugs by helping define new disease states for that purpose and encouraging off-label uses. They have been rushing harmful medical devices and drugs to the market, and hurting their customers for their short-term benefit. But what everybody is forgetting is that consumer spending constitutes 70% of this economy, and if you kill your customers (whether physically or figuratively), you won't have any economy, you won't have a stock market, and you won't have any stocks or stock prices to worry about. That's what I mean by saying every system has in it the seeds of its own demise. Some people might argue that if these companies sell their wares globally, then consumer spending will not matter much. But in reality, it should still matter because how can you have a good life if your house is falling apart?

We have witnessed the collapse of Communism. If what I have described above is not policed and kept in check, then it will bring about the collapse of Capitalism as we know it.

OUR WORLD IS THOUGHTS

About the laws, again, we did not create any of these laws. We are just a part of the whole. We have been given the capability to understand a lot of it. Will we ever be able to understand all of it? We can only strive to do so as much as possible. Some things will always be above our understanding because our form limits us as human beings. For example, we will never know where our spirit comes from or where it goes after it leaves our human body, or if it will exist outside our human body at all. Therefore, there will always be something we can't know.

Then you might ask: what is our spirit? Our spirit is part of the big spirit that is the all. Me, my spirit, I am the result of the sum of the essence that makes me alive, my genetic influences, and my experiences–that's what forms my equation. But, if I had an identical twin or a clone with the same genetic code as mine, her equation would not be the same as mine because her experiences and her thoughts generated by those experiences will always be different from mine. That makes my spirit different from hers. Therefore, my spirit inhabits my body, and develops depending on my body's genetics (which might not be unique to me) and my thoughts (which are always unique to me). That makes what "I am" equal to what my thoughts are. I am my "thoughts," and my thoughts are a part of all thoughts.

To me, I am my thoughts. To you, I am the thoughts you have of me.

Therefore, a human becomes his own being whenever he/she starts developing thoughts.

Does that happen when we are still in the womb? EEGs have been done on fetuses and there is still controversy over whether actual brainwaves have been picked up from them. The answer to this quest is still an ongoing debate between "pro-choicers" and "pro-lifers." An EEG machine can pick up our thoughts in the form of brainwaves. That's the way we determine if anybody is still alive when we are not sure. We do an EEG, and when their thoughts stop, and there are no more brainwaves detected, we determine that they have died even if their bodies are still attached to life supporting machines that keep them going.

Let's stay on that topic for a minute because I have a very important thing to tell the "pro-lifers": a fetus is a part of the mother's body, and nobody has any rights over it other than the mother herself. If we did have the right to protect it, then we should be able to put that mother in chains to prevent her from smoking, drinking alcohol, and doing drugs. We should be able to force her to sleep as much time as she should, eat only what is good for the fetus, and not engage in any activities that might jeopardize its health and life in any way, shape or form. We should be able to prevent her from having sex with people who might give her an STD, and we should be able to lock her up in isolation to prevent her from getting any communicable disease, and so on and so forth… I think you do get the gist of what I'm trying to say. What

I'm saying is that we cannot protect the fetus, but if we really care about it, we should take care of its mother's wellbeing. If we do this well, that mother might decide not to abort it, but if the mother's wellbeing is in jeopardy, and she is forced to keep it, then the fate of that baby might be worse than death.

Now let's go back to my original topic. At the time of my body's death, my developed spirit will never be present the same way ever in life as we know it again because it has lost my body, because my body is the equipment needed to generate my thoughts. But, it would have changed the course of life forever by the way it would have affected the people and events around me, and how that would have changed the way these people affected the people around them, and so on and so forth... That is true for every spirit on the face of this earth. Our thoughts will continue to affect the future that way.

To us, we're afraid that we will cease to exist when we die, when our story ends. We're afraid that our memories of ourselves cease and end and are gone forever. We have one chance during our lifetime to form memories, and our lives are about those we form. That's why when your loved ones develop advanced Alzheimer's disease, you feel as if they have already died. To the other people around us, our lives are about the memories they have of us while we are alive, and those they keep after we die. When my father was in California, and I was in Kansas City, my father was the memories I had of him. After my father died, he remained as the memories I have of him. The only difference is that I am not forming any more new ones.

So is this the only way that we will continue to live on? Will our thoughts stop when our bodies stop, or will they continue to develop in another realm and in another form? Everything's possible, but we will never know for sure. Never! Therefore our knowledge will always be limited. What I know is that we are alive because we have something to do; when we don't have anything to do anymore and no more purpose in life, we die.

Therefore, when you're alive, do something.

Our body dies, but we are not just our bodies. Our bodies are the vehicles we use during our lifetime. We come to identify ourselves with our bodies and we should, because our thoughts about the way our bodies look and feel are variables in our equation, and affect our spirit. But parts of our equation are also our ideas, thoughts and memories from our experiences. When we add that up together, we realize that all parts of our equation are about our thoughts! Our world is "thoughts." The world is "thoughts." Thoughts are electric discharges in our nervous system. That is what we are and that is what it is.

Our thoughts can be picked up as brainwaves by an EEG machine, and everything we know in life is coming at us in the form of vibrating waves. The solid structures we see have been translated into waves that travel and enter our eyes, and generate electrical impulses that travel to our brain centers, which then translate them into thoughts of a picture or a structure. The sounds we hear and the

smells we perceive are thoughts generated by waves
that enter our ears and noses. That means that all the
information in these waves actually exists in the air around
us. It is encoded by different frequencies of vibrations
and different concentrations. Then the receptors in our
bodies are equipped to translate these different waves'
frequencies and concentrations into our complex reality,
as we know it. The touch and the taste and all our feelings
are also thoughts generated by sensory impulses traveling
to our brains. The taste of food is like musical notes.
Geometry is solid music.

A feeling is a thought associated with bodily effects.
For example, a thought of feeling good or bad could make
you smile or frown; similarly, bodily effects like smiling
or frowning could generate a thought of feeling good
or feeling bad. That's why "biofeedback" and "cognitive
retraining" work. So, if something makes you feel bad, and
you decide to change the effect on your body and smile
instead of frown, that in turn will make you feel good. For
example, when you're happy, you smile because whatever
gave you the thought of being happy caused your body to
smile. Now, if you feel sad and unhappy, smile. Yes. Force
yourself to smile and see what that will do for you. That
bodily effect usually associated with the ideas of happiness
will trigger those positive thoughts in your brain. You will
automatically trick your brain into thinking you're happy,
and that will generate in you feelings of wellbeing. Go
ahead and smile now! Smile.

When you experiment with controlling your thoughts
that way, and you become good at it, you will be able to

control other bodily functions as well. You will be able to slow your heart rate and lower your blood pressure, control anxiety and eliminate fear, etc. That's how you become captain of your destiny.

And here, I'm going to stress that metaphor I have used when I said you become "captain" of your destiny, because that is the best way to explain how you can achieve control in life by controlling your thoughts. You won't be able to control the weather you're navigating in, or the seas, but you can educate yourself to learn how to avoid bad weather and bad seas, and how to steer your ship the best way possible and get it to your destination. Go ahead, be brave, educate yourself and steer, you're in the captain's position.

Life is about waking up every morning to be brave and tackle the problems of that day. Even if everything is going well with all of your affairs, you might end up having a leaking faucet that you will have to deal with. Always keep some money aside to deal with a leaking faucet day, and then deal with it. Solve your problems. Don't run away from them using drugs and alcohol. Drugs and alcohol will never stop your faucet from leaking. Also, they will interfere with your ability to form new memory, and to accumulate new knowledge and grow. Memory is what we need to rely on to solve bigger problems in our future, and to help us heal emotionally and physically. You want to heal from your addiction? Bring back your memory from the time when you were clean, and remember how things inside and outside your body felt to your senses, when you were not in a "fog." Restoring that memory is one of the main things that will help you heal.

Another metaphor that might explain to you how you can steer your life when you control your thoughts is treating your mind like a horse, i.e. if your mind wants to go right into bad thoughts, give it a kick with your horse spurs and make it go left into good thoughts instead. Tell yourself to stop it and force yourself to think and do something else. Instead of wallowing in your sorrow, think about something you enjoy and do something you enjoy. I'm not telling you anything you haven't heard before; everybody knows to look at the "glass half full rather than half empty," and everybody knows to "think positive and not negative," and to "look on the bright side."

Yes, you can do that. It works! Try it. It might be difficult at the beginning, but the more you do that exercise, the easier it gets. Yes, it's a mental exercise and your brain is like a muscle–the more you exercise it, the stronger it gets. The more you exercise your willpower, the better it gets.

Now I'm not saying that you should never wallow in your sorrow. We all need to do that every once in a while. Why? It's because it feels good. We all need to cycle. We can't stay happy all the time; it will cause strain the same way it would if you keep your back straight constantly. We all need to feel bad for ourselves for a moment, and have somebody else feel compassion for us. If it didn't feel good to wallow, then nobody would have wallowed, but don't overdo it! People will feel compassionate for you for a minute, but then they will get tired of it. So go ahead and feel sorry for yourself for a little bit, then pick

yourself back up. Nobody can pick you up but yourself.
The more you pick yourself up, the easier it gets. Just
like keeping your back straight, you will need to relax
every once in a while, then straighten up, then relax,
then straighten back up again. The more you do that
exercise, the better you will get at it. Using drugs or
alcohol to make you "high" when you're "low" will prevent
you from being able to do that exercise, will prevent
you from becoming more capable, and will arrest your
mental development. Life is full of problems. They are
everywhere to be had every day. The more skilled you get
at controlling your thoughts, the better your ability will
be to solve them. Then, the more problems you solve,
the easier it will be to solve more and more and bigger
problems—your brain becomes more capable.

The Serenity Prayer states, "God grant me the
serenity to accept the things I cannot change, courage
to change the things I can, and wisdom to know the
difference." But, how can we figure out whether we can
change something or not without trying first? We can't.
Therefore, we should always try to change what needs to
be changed. If we succeed, then so be it. If not, then we
can't blame ourselves for not trying—we accept and move
on. That's the only way! I'll explain it this way: even if
I cannot change any other variable in the equation I'm
presented with, I should always be capable of changing
one—my reaction. By changing my reaction, I would still
have a chance at changing the outcome. For example,
somebody wants to make me mad and I don't get mad,
then that somebody has failed.

Therefore, we might not be able to control what happens to us in life, but we should always be able to control our reaction to it, and by doing that, we might be able to change the outcome. So "control yourself."

VIBRATING WAVES AND PROPORTIONS

J ust like our receptors perceive vibrating waves, all
other animals also have receptors that perceive different
waves. Some animals can detect waves that our receptors
don't—like dogs, whose ears hear a different wave
spectrum than ours. Whales can navigate the vast oceans
in straight lines because they have receptors that allow
them to perceive those straight lines. Similarly, albatrosses,
monarch butterflies and pigeons navigate the airwaves
to reach their certain destinations because of what they
perceive with their special receptors. That information is
encoded in waves around us everywhere.

Therefore, it's all about vibrating waves and
wavelengths that constitute forces. Everything depends on
the wave as the main event or force, and more specifically
the frequency and concentration of the waves, i.e. the
proportion. Everything is relative to the proportion—for
example, a little more frequency generates a different
color, a different note, a different taste, etc.

I'll elaborate more about proportions here, and the fact
that life depends on proportions. Embryos of vertebrates
start with the same blueprint, and develop into different
species because their separate parts develop into different
proportions relative to each other. That's how smart the
system is! That way, the law is set once and everything

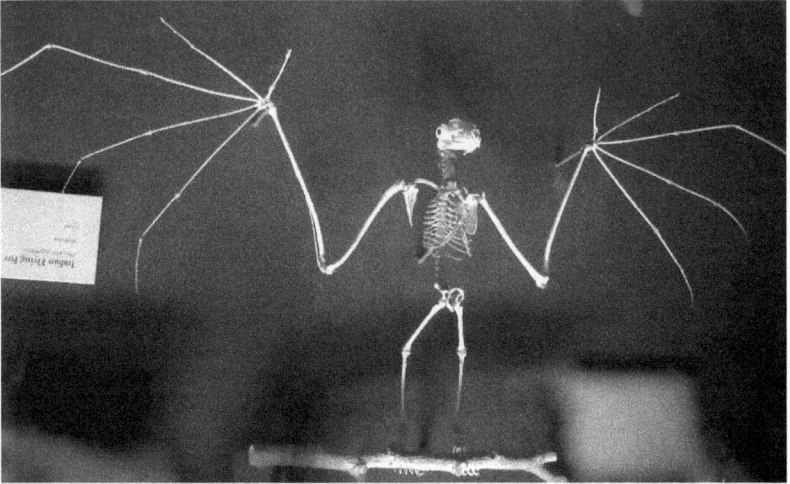

BAT SKELETON IMAGE BY GET DIRECTLY DOWN.

ensues from that law. For example, a bat's skeleton is similar to that of a human being's, but the proportion of all of the bones to each other varies. So is it a coincidence that fictions about men changing into vampire bats intrigue us, or is it our smart subconscious that realizes that it is just a matter of proportions and not that far fetched?

Proportions also determine the variety of peoples' looks. For example, Africans generally have more round bodies where the proportion of the depth to the width is bigger than for Caucasians. Thus Caucasians bodies are more flat. Asians have even more flat bodies… Now somebody might say this is racist! Yes, exactly, it is. That's exactly why races exist. Similarly, the difference between one face and the other is the proportion of one feature to the other: the distance from the hairline to the eyebrow level relative to the distance from the eyebrow level to the eyes, relative to the length of the nose, the length of the chin, the width of the face, the fullness of the lips, etc. That's why you see some brothers like the Baldwin brothers for example, or sisters that look so much alike, and yet one of them is more attractive than the other one. It's not because the face of the more attractive one is better proportioned by a certain standard of proportions! No. It's because the features of the more attractive face are better proportioned relative to each other. That's why a narrow face might not need a narrow nose, and a more rounded nose will give it an impression of more fullness. And that's why most plastic surgeries end up messing up people's looks, because it takes a genius artist to be able to figure out what the best proportions for a particular face are, and those artists are rare. Similar rules apply to the proportions of the bodies. Plastic surgeons should stick to correcting gross deformities only because the majority of them are not good artists.

Therefore our lives are about the vibrating waves that form the thoughts and the essence that makes us alive. When our thoughts and understanding become well developed, we can achieve a point where our "vibes" can become in harmony with the rest of the Universe. That's when we start discovering and inventing new things. Inventors often describe the process of inventing as an epiphany or revelation. But that happens only after we have accumulated enough knowledge and understanding, and not before.

Another phenomenon happens when our waves are resonating with the waves around us. We start experiencing unrelated events occurring to us by chance in a very meaningful manner. That's the phenomenon that some people term as "synchronicity." Carl Gustav Jung first described the concept of synchronicity in the 1920s. Some people call it an intervention of grace. When synchronicity is happening to us, it means that we are on the right track. That's the best explanation I could come up with for that phenomenon. What else?

I have experienced some episodes of synchronicity–I was driving down an unfamiliar road in Liberty, Missouri one day, then I stopped at a stoplight while listening to a story on the radio talking about a crystal hanging in the window of a house that ended up concentrating enough sunlight in one spot to light the house on fire. I looked up

and saw that the name of the road where I was stopped is
Lightburne!

Another example is when, after picking up my
daughter from school, and hearing about some injustice
that she had experienced that day, we both agreed that "life
sucks sometimes," only to turn around the corner, and find
ourselves behind a car with the license plate: "LIFSGR8!"
Did we end up having big smiles on our faces then? Of
course, we did!

These episodes started happening to me with an
increased frequency, so I couldn't help but realize that
there must be a meaning to all of this. Prior to that, when
they occurred every once in a while, I dismissed them
as "coincidence." But when these "coincidences" started
becoming more and more frequent, it hit me in the face,
and I couldn't help but realize that there must be some
mechanism of action that was generating them. I am
certain a big number of you have had similar experiences
also. To the ones who haven't had them yet, pay attention
and you will notice because sooner or later it will happen
to you too.

That raises the following question: If we can be in
harmony with the vibes of the universe when we are on
the right track, could we be in dissonance with the vibes
when we are not, and bring upon ourselves the wrath of
dissonance? Religions have warned us about the wrath of
God, and that it will be a consequence for our bad actions.
Their sayings have been ridiculed. But could they have
been right? Are we bringing damage upon ourselves by the
kind of actions we are taking, our bad vibes?

Here is one specific example of how we can be on the right wavelength. It's from my personal experience, and it might correspond to examples from your life. I was driving down a two-way street when I came across a car accident that had just occurred. A flatbed trailer had just come loose from the back of a vehicle, and slammed into the front of a small sized car behind it, with a young girl in the driver's seat. I parked my car out of the way and stepped out to see if I could help. I assessed the situation before the paramedics arrived. The accident was serious. The dashboard had slammed into the girl's knees and she was not coherent, which meant to me that she had suffered a serious injury. The paramedics arrived and had to use the Jaws of Life to extricate her from her seat. When they were putting her on the stretcher, I prevented them from straightening her legs out, and instructed them to keep them the way they were—bent at the hips and the knees—and to strap her in that position because I figured that some of her bones were broken. And I went on my way. I was thankful I was there because it was going to be more damaging to the girl to forcibly straighten her legs out, and I helped avoid that from happening. A couple of years later, I was driving down a two-way street. A car ahead of me was pulling a flatbed, when suddenly and totally out of the blue, the flatbed came loose and started bouncing backwards towards me. At the speeds we were all traveling there was nothing I could have done to avoid a head-on collision, nothing! I realized that, when suddenly, the flatbed started bouncing on its right-sided wheels, and towards the right of me and completely out of my way, as if by magic! All that unfolded before I could flinch, and a certain disaster was averted.

Here is another specific example of how we can be in dissonance. It's about a friend who was dumped by her fiancé when her brother was diagnosed with schizophrenia because her fiancé became worried that, knowing this condition can be hereditary, they might end up having a schizophrenic child. More than ten years pass; he gets married and makes sure to tell my friend that his wife was from a good genetic stock. They have their first child together who had a genetic abnormality that the doctors were not even familiar with!

What the examples above show is how things in life seem to work within a certain order. First of all, our actions are never forgotten. Second, we don't just get paid back, but we get "paid back in kind." It wasn't just a disaster for a disaster; it was for the same exact kind of disaster using the same tools! The Collective Subconscious has already determined the existence of that phenomenon as the concept of karma. People readily acknowledge it as a fact that: "What goes around comes around!"

Everybody is aware of that phenomenon happening to us at our scale as human beings. That doesn't mean that if you do something bad, something bad will happen to you right away as a payback. Sometimes that occurs; at other times, it might take a while. But one thing is for certain though: sooner or later, we will get paid back. In some instances as the ones described earlier, events transpire in a way that forces us to realize that, "At our scale, we are special, and the universe is ours." Some people will feel that a message is being relayed, and that they are being watched and rewarded or punished by God, but the scientific explanation for that phenomenon is resonance and dissonance.

Does that mean that we are bringing natural disasters upon ourselves by collectively being out of sync with the vibes of the Universe, when we are generating bad vibes? Are our bad actions causing earthquakes and volcanoes to erupt and tsunamis, etc? No they are not because at any particular time, the collective human beings' behavior all throughout the generations is the same. You always have the greedy and the thieves and the righteous and the good and the bad and the war and the peace, etc. Because of that, we can accurately conclude that natural disasters happen randomly, and not as a result of human beings' collective behavior. We also should not forget that our actions are just a minute fraction in the big equation of all of the variables that have to come together to cause natural disasters to happen. Therefore, in our world at our scale, the vibes we generate pay us back. But, on the large scale of things, we are only a part of the multitude. Our bad vibes, for example, are not going to cause a natural disaster to happen that will end up killing all the innocent animals also. No! We are not that important.

So does God cause natural disasters to happen? Natural disasters happen because of scientific reasons. As stated above, when we don't understand the science, we call it God. But since God is everything including the science, then we can say that God causes natural disasters to happen. It's just a matter of semantics! Why do you not want to have respect for God? You don't want to have fear? I understand that. But does it make it less fearsome to know that when it rains stones from the sky, it is the wrath of meteorites and not the wrath of God? Or is it less fearsome to see New Orleans flooding because of the hurricane and failure of the levies and not the wrath of God? There should still be fear and respect. Don't you fear a volcano? Don't you fear a tsunami, a hurricane, a tornado, and large meteor showers? Epidemics? Earthquakes? We always fear these calamities. We can stop fearing them only when we can control them, and up until now, we haven't been able to. We have been trying, but have not succeeded yet. In addition to the human loss, a lot of damage from the New Orleans flooding was done to our pride because of the failure of our advanced science and technology. Can we stop a hurricane or a tornado from striking, and prevent the devastation that ensues? Our science has failed us thus far.

Therefore, our bad vibes do not cause natural disasters to happen on the large scale, but they do have consequences on our smaller scale. When we want to control and become so powerful and almighty and arrogant, we end up getting out of tune with the universe, and bring damage upon ourselves—we get "humbled." We forget that our good will not continue to exist at the expense of the good of people around us, and at the expense of the all.

EVERYTHING MOVES

Now, let's go back to the subject of vibes. Everything vibrates, everything moves. In physics, it is well known that matter is nothing more than the geometric distribution of forces in space. The forces create atoms that create molecules that create larger structures that move. Everything in this world exhibits motion at its own time scale. For example, electrons vibrate in atoms and molecules, and plants and animals grow from dust and then are returned to dust again. Rivers and seas and oceans are in constant movement and water circulates to and back from the atmosphere. The crust of earth moves during earthquakes, hot magma comes out from inside the earth through volcanoes, rocks move and are formed and crumble... Earth and all of our planets move around the sun. The solar system and the stars are moving in the Milky Way Galaxy. All of the galaxies are moving in an expanding universe... Everything moves.

We will not perceive all of these movements when we are observing from our perspective using our own time scale, but if we could change the speed of our time, we would be able to. I will give you examples in what follows.

If we change our time scale, and decide that our "one day" consists of a whole rotation of the earth around the sun instead of around itself, then we will see the movement of the rocks and earth's crust speed up. That's what I mean when I say "time from our perspective," because time as we know it depends on the size of our earth, and how long it takes for it to revolve around itself and the sun. This time is relative to us. That means it is "relative" and not absolute. Outside our earth, time is different. For example, a day on Jupiter is closer to 10 hours to our 24, while a year on Jupiter is close to 12 years on earth. That means if we lived on Jupiter, our average lifetime as human beings, which is 78 Earth years, would become 78 divided by 12 of Jupiter years, which is 6.5 Jupiter years. But when we measure time, we always measure it from the perspective of our Earth and our life expectancy. That's why to us, 2011 years since Jesus Christ seems to be an eternity.

Therefore, what we have been concerned with during our lives is what is relevant to us at our scale. We have measured everything relative to our size on our earth. For example, a yard or a foot or a year ... A year is the time it takes for our earth to make a whole rotation around the sun. But let's think about things a little differently for a moment. Let's do another mental exercise and look at the Earth and human life from a different perspective—that 10,000 years of our earthly years are equal to "one minute" in the different perspective. If that were the case, then all Homo sapiens would have existed for 5 to 20 "minutes," which means we have all existed at the same time. And if we look at it from the perspective of our story as human beings, we find that it is in fact the same. It is true that technology changes, but the human story does not change at all: in every society, you always have the rich and the less rich and the poor and the tug of war between the classes; you always have the tug of war between the sexes, and the generations. You always have the experts and the scientists and the laborers and the fathers and the mothers and the crooks and the murderers, etc. You always have similar dynamics between people. You always have the latest technologies. What used to be a pony express to relay information becomes a telegram that becomes a telephone that becomes a videophone … What used to be building pyramids becomes building skyscrapers … That's what the difference is: using different tools to achieve the same goals–in this instance, relay information and build edifices. But the rest of the story remains the same, and keeps repeating over and over.

When you become aware of that fact, you will realize that you can recognize the past, and you can recognize the future as if you've actually lived them. If you watch a movie set during those time periods, you will notice that the human emotions and dynamics are always the same, and the events; happy and tragic effects are the same also. Therefore, you really don't need to live more into the future, you just need to live your life now and realize the universality of it, and how valuable it is–for it is a window on eternity.

WORDS ARE METAPHORS

What this last chapter demonstrates is how changing the semantics can free and broaden our understanding, and how words are actual metaphors. That's why I am trying to explain to you how things work in our earthly life, as we know it, using today's science metaphor. I am not going to tell you anything new that you haven't heard before. I will use facts that people who went to high school know and understand, and put these facts together in a way that will shed a new light on life's issues, making everything clearer and more understandable to the majority of people. Some people have been doing research and analyzing how things in life work and studying the trees. In here, I'm going to put that knowledge together, and help you see the forest.

I'll show you how everything can be explained using equations constructed like a chemical equation to study the forces of physics at play, and a mathematical equation to include all of the variables involved. It's a very simple and beautiful answer that helps us understand the complexities of life.

But first, what do I mean when I say all words are metaphors? Words are metaphors that we use to explain what one person thinks or feels with his senses to the rest of the people, trying to relay his truth to them in the most accurate way possible. Because once we choose a word to describe something, that immediately puts a limit on what we're trying to describe, and it distorts the truth. That makes the word we use a metaphor of the real thing, i.e. a symbol. For example, if we try to describe a color as being red, but in reality, this color has a hint of white in it making it a pinkish red, it makes calling it red inaccurate. But we call it red anyway. That color will be different from a second red with a hint of brown in it that we also refer to as red, and this second red color will in turn be different from a third red color that has a little more brown in it. Now, if we put these three different red colors next to each other, our eye recognizes the difference immediately, but when we have to use words to relay what the eye is seeing, we use the word "red" for all three colors, which becomes a symbol of what we're seeing: a metaphor. If we want to be more accurate and closer to the truth, we can say one red has a hint of white in it and the second one has a hint of brown in it and a third one has more brown in it. But as Pantone Colors says, there are literally millions of colors, and as everybody knows, we do not have millions of names for them. So if we want to be more accurate in describing a color, we can try to do that, but we will never succeed. That fact proves one thing, and that is that the word red is only a metaphor, and the use of that metaphor distorts the truth. When that same thinking process is applied to all the other words that we use, we become aware of the limitations of every word. Usually we take words as being truths by themselves for the sake of rapid communication of ideas, and in general, they do serve the purpose, but if we want to be more accurate, those words fail.

Words fail the most when we're trying to explain or to understand a completely novel process. That's why seeing what is being described makes the transfer of information a whole lot easier and more accurate. When I was a new medical student studying medicine for the first time, I would read the books and have a hard time understanding the technical words, for example "dry scaly scab" or "pitting edema." But once I did get the chance to see what's being described, I would understand very quickly. That's why education should not rely on books alone, because there is no replacing what can be learned from what the eye can see, and what the senses can perceive. What the eye sees in a fraction of a second, and what the brain processes during that time, could take many pages to describe accurately with words. That means if you have a good eye and a critical mind, you can learn a lot. And that's what actually happens in real life: as long as we're alive, we're learning.

That same thinking process applies to mathematical symbols. They are nothing more than metaphors to symbolize whole descriptive processes. For example, delta refers to the difference between two values. Now, since the male brain thinks differently from the female brain, and males are more tuned into using symbols (Gurian, 2001), that helps explain why more males are more apt at math—and as a result of that, don't get discouraged by it. In order to have more women become interested in math, we need to use less symbols and use more descriptive words, for example instead of using delta, use "difference in between." That will slow down the process, but so what?

Putting timing on solving math equations is the most useless thing I have ever seen in my life, and the speed relies mostly on memory. It's just another man's way of flexing muscle and showing off, and does not serve any other purpose whatsoever. What really matters in math is to be able to understand the concepts and the logic, and to be able to problem solve.

Therefore, to describe something, we use metaphors like in the medical language, the math language, the engineering language … These metaphors become the impediment to learning. Most of the time spent specializing in a subject is spent learning the language of that subject. The concepts themselves are actually easy and any normal brain will be able to understand them, which is exactly what ends up happening in reality, after the language is mastered. We create a language to communicate, and it becomes the monster that we have to tame and in a lot of instances, it becomes the obstacle.

DIMENSIONS AND REALITY

You might not have been aware that words are metaphors and do not represent absolute truths. What you also might not have been aware of is that you have no idea what you look like in real life. That is because what you see when you look at yourself is your two-dimensional image in a mirror or on a screen. You see an illusion of what your reality is. You can never see yourself the way you are in real life in three dimensions while moving and talking, which is the way that everybody else sees you. What you know about the way you look is a composite idea you build in your brain when you look at your image from different angles. So it is an approximation of what you actually look like. To the other people that see you in 3D moving and talking and emitting vibes, you are different. Nowadays in our culture, we have come to uphold 2D illusions of people's looks as representative of the ideals of beauty when they don't even belong to the reality at all whatsoever. We have heard about photogenic people. What does it mean when somebody is photogenic? It means that they look better in their 2D picture than in their 3D reality. Usually these people have angular features that end up delineating their looks for the camera, and not blending the planes of the sides of their face with the front of their face as much as people with more round features do. People with more round features' pictures give the illusion that their faces are fatter. The same thing applies to pictures of bodies when the planes of their sides blend in with their front, thus giving the illusion that they are fatter. That's why everybody has realized that pictures add pounds to your appearance. That phenomenon has caused anorexia, eating disorders, and plastic surgeries, which is a significant problem plaguing our day and age.

Studying how illusions work in 2D allows the skilled artist to manipulate images to show whatever that person wants. That phenomenon has resulted in the ideal of beauty being hijacked, distorted and used to control people. That has led some to mutilate their bodies and cause disease and death for the purpose of achieving an ideal 2D image of themselves: a good-looking illusion!

Wake up people, and remember what real beauty is. Haven't we all met that particular person that impressed us in the first few seconds as being ugly, only to have us change our mind as soon as he/she starts emitting sounds and moving, and we never see them as ugly anymore ever again? And the same thing is true vice-versa: haven't we all met that beautiful person that is not as beautiful as soon as they move or open their mouths? Also, people want to emulate a certain ideal of beauty. They do things that threaten their lives and could distort their looks forever to look like a certain celebrity or the other. Why? If everybody looked alike, there would be sameness. We would come to know what to expect and become not interested to look. There won't be any more beauty! On the other hand, new intriguing features make us want to look some more. What's beautiful is when we have diversity because that keeps life more interesting.

PERFECTION IS IN THE IMPERFECTION!

Yes, perfection is in the imperfection. That's what the scientists who have been trying to define ideals for a perfect society with perfect human beings need to realize. They just need to look around and understand how things work in real life. Every single human being has an invaluable role they play to make us all whole. Even dependant people serve to make us slow down, and become more humble and less arrogant, and therefore make us better human beings. Nature also gives us all the viable varieties possible to ensure that, if some new disease strikes the population, there would be a better chance to have somebody survive the disaster. That way, redundancy is built into the system. A good example is how people with Sickle-cell Disease are immune to Malaria.

Some other people think that they can breed beautiful people to get beautiful descendents. But things don't work out that way. Just look at the good-looking movie stars who marry beautiful people. It seems that quite often, their grown children are lacking in the looks department as compared to them. On the other hand, if you're watching a beauty pageant and you see these beautiful girls, you feel shocked when the cameras pan out into the audience to show you the parents, and you can't help but wonder how people with such average looks can have such beautiful children!

In reality, what it boils down to in the long run is that superficial beauty as manipulated by the camera is about youth and good health. Don't forget that age evens out the beauty playing field, and as we age, we can't help but look back at the young people in wonder of how beautiful they all are. But deep beauty that is captured by all our senses is about the smartness, goodness and decency that emanate in our vibes. That is what real beauty is because what goes on inside of you shows on your face.

A third reality you might not have been aware of is that nothing in real life exists in 2D. When your image is a 2D representation of you in 3D; the actual picture is made with an ink layer that has three dimensions. For example, when you draw a line with a pencil on a piece of paper, that line has a length and a width, but it also has a depth because of the microscopic thickness of the lead on the paper. It appears as if it is 2-dimensional relative to our senses, but in reality it is 3-dimensional. But then you might say, "My image is in 2D." Yes it is. But images are optical illusions and they never capture the 3D reality. It takes an extremely skilled artist to be able to depict an image that is very close to the 3D reality, but it will never be totally exact. So that begs the next question: does anything in real life exist in 2D? Not really, only illusions exist in 2D, because if we go down to the atomic level, it is three-dimensional also.

Nowadays, our world is becoming more and more filled with 2D illusions because of the way we have incorporated electronic images into our daily lives. But, since our world is all about our thoughts, then that makes our two-dimensional illusions very important aspects of our reality.

GOOD AND BAD

We live with the illusions of an unreal 2D world, but is that a new thing? No it's not, because mind illusions have always been a huge part of human beings' lives. The best example is how people take words that are actual metaphors as being actual truths. They lend themselves to becoming easily manipulated by the words of whoever HIJACKS THE RHETORIC. Everybody knows to judge based on the actions and not the words, but most people don't do that. They end up living in a world of illusions. Also, people start their lives as very romantic beings, and more sensitive to the magic of their world, which makes it more beautiful. They believe all that they hear. They believe in abstract notions like good vs. bad, romanticism without materialism, and eternal love, etc. For example, children believe all other human beings are good, and that nobody will hurt them, until they get hurt. They wake up to the real three-dimensional world and become more concrete only after major events strike them in their lives. They start wondering how come people can be bad to them for no obvious reason, and they might decide to take revenge and be bad in return.

But how do we define "who" is good and "who" is bad? It's not as easy as it seems, and here's a perfect example: How is it that a woman who sleeps with one person who might be her husband, who cheats on her, exposes her to

STDs and treats her badly is a good woman? On the other hand, how is it that a woman who sleeps with several people who treat her badly and expose her to STDs is a bad woman? How does that definition hold? What is the bad part exactly? Is the sex the bad part? —Because both women are having sex. Both women are getting screwed physically and figuratively, which is supposed to be what's bad in these two equations, and both women are not being good to themselves. Our society seems to define good and bad in such ways that seem to muddy the picture, and yet, as it turns out, society's definition is actually correct because the Collective Subconscious knew the real truth all along.

The real truth is that the woman who has her partner's interest at heart and does not cheat on him is the good person, and the woman who sleeps around and does not hold anybody's interest at heart is the bad person.

The Collective Subconscious has defined a good person as the one who is good to others, and the bad person as the one who isn't. How did it come to a decision of that sort? It's because what's good for me is good until it becomes bad for you, or vice versa. Based on that assertion, it becomes clear that I would be considered to be a good person only if I hold your interest at heart, and looking at it from that perspective, we can deduce that those who have other people's interest at heart are good people, and those who don't are bad people.

The other reason is that doing good deeds is the only thing that will make you feel goodness, because you feel love only when you love, and you feel goodness only when you "do good." Those of you who have experienced that feeling of goodness know what I'm talking about. To all the others, the proof is in how the idiom "for goodness' sake" has been widely adopted, even though some of its users have not been consciously aware of its true meaning. But its meaning has actually been clarified in the lyric "so be good for goodness' sake" from one of the most popular songs ever: "Santa Claus is coming to town." And what it means is that you ought to be good to others, so that you will know what goodness feels like, because that will be better for you. Everybody has readily adopted that expression because the subconscious has been aware of that mechanism of action all along.

Bad people who are only focused on their own good do not feel love for you, and do not experience the feeling of goodness. You can love them and do all kinds of good things for them because you love them, but they perceive it as dependence or sucking up because you are inferior and they are better than you. They will not feel your love and if they don't learn how to love, they will never feel love, period. If they don't learn how to be good to others, they will never feel goodness either. They might get rich; they might buy cars and trucks, houses and yachts. People will admire them, but how will that make them feel? Powerful and almighty maybe, but that's all.

Good people feel love and goodness, which generates content and happiness, even when they are not rich. Because they are content, their souls are at peace, and that is priceless. You cannot buy these feelings with money.

Everybody knows that. Everybody and their mothers know that "money can't buy happiness."

A good spouse or partner is one who has your interest at heart–the one who realizes that your good is their good. A good person can sacrifice for their spouse or children or employer or friend, not because they are dumb, but because first of all, it makes them feel goodness to be good, and second, they figure out that it might pay back in the future. I call that being long-sited and smart-selfish. A mother can sacrifice for her children, for example, and help them become independent successful human beings, so that they don't remain dependent on her in the future, and she might need their help for something someday. A bad person looks at what's good for them right now, even at the expense of what's good for everybody else in the future, including themselves. I call that being short-sited and dumb-selfish.

The ideal situation develops between two people when they are in harmony, on the same wavelength, the same page: when they have each other's interests at heart.

To sum it all up, in the long run, and on the large scale of things, what is good for me is when I feel goodness when I do good. But in the process of doing that, I should also protect myself from the bad people who don't have my interest at heart. In the real world, what ends up happening is a tug of war between what's good for me against what's good for you, if what's good for you is not good for me.

It all depends on the conflict of interest!

What is bad for me is when the scales get tipped for you at my expense. When things become more good for you than for me, the forces start developing to correct that imbalance. More and more forces develop until the balance is improved. That is what we see at all scales: individuals, families, organizations, corporations, governments and countries. What ends up happening is a constant calibration and recalibration based on what is being defined as being good at any particular moment and in a particular situation. That tug of war ends up keeping things in check and balance. Because of this, you hear people voicing a clear opinion about what's good and what's bad, only to see them modify it when push comes to shove. Also, because of this, we as a human race will always end up having wars.

Now let's try to define "what" is good and "what" is bad. In reality, there is no absolute good or bad: what is good for somebody could be considered bad for the other. What it becomes in the majority of peoples' minds depends on just that: the majority, the proportion. That's how a small group of armed people becomes a militia, and a larger proportion becomes an army. And that's why, HIJACKING THE RHETORIC to sway the opinion of the general public using the most powerful PR machine on the face of this earth has always been the most essential aspect of the Israeli/Palestinian conflict, thus trying to blind people from seeing the "actual proportion" of casualties and damage doled out. In the process of doing that, everybody is forgetting that Jews and Arabs are SEMITIC PEOPLE and ACTUAL COUSINS—our men have the same Y chromosome that most probably belonged to our COMMON FATHER ABRAHAM—and that WE ALL WANT PEACE!

Therefore, what's good and bad is relative, and it depends on the proportion. If the majority has their women run around naked like some tribes in Africa, then running around naked is not a bad thing. If the majority doesn't, then running around naked is a bad thing. A woman who wears a burqa for example, thinks that the woman who covers her hair and does not cover her face is doing something wrong and therefore is bad. The woman who covers her hair and skin thinks the woman who doesn't is bad. The woman who covers her bosom thinks the one who doesn't is bad and so on and so forth… Women end up deciding the slut is the one who is being more daring than them! See how it becomes relative and not absolute?

We also cannot say what's good is what has a good outcome because something bad always comes out of what's good, and what's bad is what has a bad outcome because something good always comes out of the bad. What's good and what's bad is relative and depends on the proportion. For example, a little arsenic is good because it can cure a rare form of leukemia, a little more is bad for you and will kill you. A little water is essential for life; too much water is bad for you and can kill you also. The little amount of arsenic that is good for you is a whole lot smaller than the amount of water that is good for you. Therefore, what is good and bad depends on the proportion of the actual thing in question. That makes it safer for us to handle water for example, as compared to arsenic. Similarly, when Columbian people chew on coca leaves, they get the benefit of cocaine in minuscule amounts as opposed to people who use cocaine in a more concentrated powder form and develop addictions and sickness as a result of it. The same applies to alcohol and all other substances including narcotics. A little alcohol can be good for you, a little more causes disease. A little narcotics are good for pain, too much narcotics cause tolerance to develop and create addictions and don't work for pain anymore, even resulting in Opioid-induced Hyperalgesia, which results in more and more pain.

Religions tend to define what's relatively good or bad as absolute good or bad. All religions are relatively good. One thing that is bad is what some people make of religion, and when they tell their followers that everybody else is bad. Sometimes those beliefs cause war because they can tip the scale and disrupt the balance. Relatively bad people (that we refer to as bad people) will not be guided by anything, and they will use everything to their own benefit at the expense of everybody else's, including religion. On the other hand, relatively good people (that we refer to as good people) use religion to strengthen their own beliefs.

In reality, life is so hard and can bring out what's bad in people. Without religion, there would be more badness, because life is difficult and complicated, and it is easy to lose the way. Religion exists because people need it; if it was not useful it wouldn't have existed in the past, and it wouldn't have continued to exist until now. If there were no religion, we would have invented one. And if our brain had invented it, it would still be divine because we did not invent our brain. Our brain is part of everything that is God, and it is just the conduit that is being used to relay the information needed.

Some relatively good people don't need a formal religion to be good, but does that mean they don't have religion? Even atheists have religion because they have a set belief system that they conduct their lives by.

Then we ask why do bad things happen to good people? It's because if you are good and hold other people's interest above your own at all times, you might end up being bad to yourself and make yourself vulnerable to getting hurt—and you will fall prey to the bad people who exploit your kindness. That's why it has become folk knowledge that "only the good die young," and why some cultures pity the good-hearted. It's because they might neglect their own well being right now for the sake of others while on the other hand, bad people look out for their immediate self-interest before anybody or anything. The other reason is that, when there is disease and death, bad things will happen to everybody regardless of whether these people are good or bad. Because of that, I would like to say to the bad people: be afraid because bad things happen to everybody. It's just a matter of time. Take that into consideration.

And then you might ask: why should there be pain and suffering? It's because it works in the equation of our life. It gives strength and stamina to achieve bigger things, i.e. "No pain no gain." If you want to achieve greatness, you have to take the high road, and work very hard for it—sacrifice and suffer. You have to realize that every great achievement follows a certain process and takes its own time. A successful pregnancy takes close to nine months. You go up the stairs step by step. You don't become a lawyer or doctor without spending many years in school. You don't become a successful businessman without sweating for it... You can't just sit there and think about becoming great and then you become great; the way it's been touted in the book titled "The Secret" by Rhonda Byrne! No! That's wrong! And it's not how the equation works! If it had worked out that way, then everybody would have achieved greatness already. The way the equation works is like this: you accumulate thoughts of knowledge, you add to that thoughts of action, you add to that pain and suffering and sacrifice and hard work, while at the same time, persisting in thinking that you are going to achieve greatness, and never allowing the thoughts of defeat to take over. Then you achieve greatness. That's how the formula works and not otherwise.

MONEY AND POWER

Life is difficult for everyone alike, because as long as there is disease and death, there will be difficulties... and who goes through life without getting exposed to diseases and death? Nobody! Rich people and poor people are alike. Nobody's pain is better than anybody else's. The only difference between the rich and poor is that the rich can afford more material things. That's all. But in life, owning the material things does not matter, because the Collective Subconscious knows that "money does not buy happiness." Happiness is found in the process of making money, in achieving things, in fulfilling the human ambition, and in getting in touch with the goodness within. There is nothing wrong with making money because it is the tool people agreed upon to measure achievements.

Money is a tool for survival: to eat and get health care and shelter and knowledge. But money also gives power. Common people have a lot more power than they think. In the US for example, consumer spending constitutes 70% of the nation's economy. When some politicians talk about the need for more tax breaks for "BIG BUSINESS" at the expense of the consumers, they are wrong, because it is the consumer who is driving the economy. If you kill your consumer, you have no economy! Just like in the good old days, when I sell my services to buy your eggs, and you sell your eggs to pay a doctor, and the doctor sells his services to buy my services, it makes me a businessman and my trade keeps the circulation going. If I decide to stop this circulation, you die, because when I don't sell my services to buy your eggs, you can't pay the doctor. That means it is the consumer who is the major business in the nation, the "BIGGER BUSINESS." "Big business" should know that and try to make the laws fair for everybody, but they don't. Why? It's because money becomes a tool to achieve power and to control other people. Since bad people accumulate money to have power, good people need to save money to keep the balance of power. The balance of power gets tipped easily because money and power corrupts. Corruption generates opposing forces that lead to war. That makes war necessary. When was there no war? Even Gandhi did not fight without force; he actually waged an economical war. He did not use artillery weapons, but he used economical weapons. He wielded great power when he convinced the Indians to stop all the work they were doing for the British.

The same thing applies for women: If you collectively stop giving cheap sex, you will see what your power will be like with your mates. And I'm specifying mates because women already have a lot of power over men: their sons! The collective subconscious knew that fact all along because people have always called a bad man a "Son of a Bitch." But, the worst man is the "Motherfucker" because the subconscious knows that the worst man is the one who is abnormal to the point where he could go against one of the strongest bonds in nature, and hurt even his mother.

Under normal circumstances, there is nobody on the face of this earth who will love a woman more than her son, until he finds his own mate. So, theoretically, women could wield a lot of power and change the whole world if they set themselves to do that. All that they have to do is teach their sons well. For example, they can encourage them to be good to their future mates. But that does not happen in real life, and a lot of times, the opposite will happen. Why? Again as we stated earlier, it's because what is good is relative. What is good for the son's mate might end up being bad for his mother. As I will explain later on, the boy will most probably become a provider, which will create a conflict of interest between his mother and his mate. The mate's objective is to garner all of his resources for her benefit and the benefit of her children if there are any, which might lead to the mother being left out. Even if the mother is wealthy and does not need her son's money, she might still need his resourcefulness and attention. That's why there will always be conflict between in-laws. It's because that tug of war is necessary to keep things more in balance. Men need to understand that mechanism because it will help them figure out how to draw the lines between their birth family and their married family, which will make their lives a whole lot easier when they do, and it will allow them to better navigate their married lives.

WAR

As I have stated in the earlier chapters, war is necessary to keep the balance of power between good and bad, even though war does not always need to result in bloodshed, as Gandhi has proven to us.

On the other hand, and in general, people are good and behave well. I know you will find this statement strange, but look at your teenager for example: That's the time when human beings start becoming social butterflies. Look at how well behaved your monstrous teenager is with strangers as opposed to their behavior at home. Even sociopaths are charming in public because they are so focused on what's good for them, and what's good for them starts by charming you and luring you in. Bad people usually show their badness when they are in hiding and not being watched; that's when they go for their benefit at your expense. But the social system sets itself in a way that keeps the checks and balances in order. People will always rally and create laws to stop the actions of whoever is infringing on others' good. If the majority were not really inherently good, there wouldn't have been a government force on the face of this earth that would have been able to contain their behavior. But look at them everywhere, even in the countries where most are poor (for example in the African countries or India or China, etc.); in general you see them going about their habitual activities trying to make it from day to day, and trying to get as much fun out of their day as possible. Of course war breaks out every once in a while, but considering how much conflict of interest exists between people, it is amazing that there is not war everywhere all of the time!

The same phenomenon exists at the family scale. Almost everybody comes from a family and knows the amount of conflict that goes on in each family, and yet people are not going about killing each other all the time because of this. A few do kill, but it's a minute fraction considering the amount that fight with each other. That means people have a natural built-in inhibition to kill, and the ones who don't have such an inhibition usually have a mental condition, a genetic predisposition, or they are messed up on alcohol or drugs. Also, it means that fighting is a natural thing to do—it helps create a balance between all of the forces. Because of that, it's ok to have fighting in families, and it's ok for a husband and a wife to fight, as long as the methods are not extreme and they will end up achieving a better balance. But the rules of fighting between spouses have to be honored: resolve the fight; don't escalate it, no hitting below the belt, and no hitting. Period. Now there are some that are against fighting per se, but what these people end up doing is exhibiting manipulative and passive aggressive behavior. They still generate force, but it is either a concealed force that makes it hard for you to tell where they are coming at you from or they generate a negative force.

MATHEMATICS, CHEMISTRY AND PHYSICS

In what follows, I will explain how things in life work using metaphors of mathematics, chemistry and physics. So let's go back to the subject of metaphors. To broaden our minds, and to understand what I am about to explain to you next, we should not get caught up in the semantics. Words lock things in a box, yet words can sometimes be very smart, and indicate how intelligent the Collective Subconscious is. For example, a lot of us refer to "variables" and "equations" when we are pondering a certain matter, and "patterns" and "structures" when we are discussing the workings of a specific issue (math and geometry). We also try to "do our math right," and can be "calculating" (math). We know we should "weigh our options," analyze the "dynamics" and "forces," and we are aware that "magnetism" exists between people (physics). We refer to people emitting "vibes" and being on the same "wavelength" (physics). We also talk about "chemistry" between people and "bonds" (chemistry). This proves that the Collective Subconscious has always known that things work like chemistry and physics and math. It's because the brains that we were given are smart, and know how things work even if we might not have brought that knowledge up to our conscious level.

That's what I am trying to do for you in this book. I'm going to bring that information you subconsciously knew to be true to your conscious level.

Now, for the first time, I will be putting all of these clues from the subconscious together by explaining how to look at the situation as a mathematics equation to include all variables involved, and a chemistry equation to understand what physics forces are at play. I found that everything in life could be understood better when we analyze these forces, and the geometric structures they create.

Examples of forces that compel us to behave in a certain way are: hormones, greed, envy, jealousy, love, lust, ambition, despair, pain, loyalty, faith, revenge, hate, fear, peer pressure, sibling rivalry, addictions, bonds, compassion, competition, shadenfreude, etc. When the same natural forces are put together in the same equation, they interact with each other like a chemical reaction does, leading to similar outcomes. That's how we can sometimes predict the future; e.g. when we see somebody leading a lifestyle of delinquency, indulgence in alcohol and drugs, and promiscuity, we can predict what the outcome will most probably be like.

When I started to analyze things, I noticed patterns of behavior, and after so many years, I came to the conclusion that there is a system set in place with its own rules. I will explain to you how this system operates, and why I believe the way it operates is the best way possible. When you will be able to understand and analyze things the right way, you will feel much better about life.

Patterns of behavior occur at all levels. They are the most evident when we hear jokes. For example, it is very hard not to notice that almost everybody all over the world laughs at in-law jokes. When you're having problems with your mother-in-law, and you think you're so unfortunate, I have some news for you: almost everybody with a mother-in-law has problems very similar to yours.

Patterns are also evident when we look at the universalities of some proverbs and idioms. Some proverbs stand the test of time and attest to the Universal Wisdom of the Universal Subconscious because they deliver information about natural dynamics in a small package. They ring true to everybody alike. Examples of proverbs are: "What goes up must come down," "What goes around comes around," "Too many chefs spoil the broth," "You reap what you sow," "All that glitters is not gold," "Talking is silver silence is gold."

An example of the patterns of behavior is babies growing up. Babies start to roll and sit and crawl around the same time, then they go through the terrible twos, and around age three the majority of toddlers start asking "why?" questions. Then there is the teenagers' behavior, and who does not know about that? Who does not know about the rebellion and the risky behavior that the majority of teenagers engage in to break away from their parents and their rules? Then they grow up, they marry and have kids, and more often than not the boys find themselves turning into their fathers, and the girls into their mothers.

Physics describes matter as nothing more than the geometric distribution of forces in space. I have noticed that everything in life as we know it defines structures that depend on the geometric distribution of the forces at play within. Fractally, the same laws apply on all of the different scales.

These laws apply to the structure of a company or an organization. I am sure you have seen an organizational chart drawn with the bonds clearly delineating the relationship of each member to the other, thus building its own geometric structure.

The same thing applies to the structure of a process, where you see the process algorithm drawn to depict the bonds resulting in a geometric structure of the algorithm.

And again in a family, forces define the "family structure," which takes a certain geometric shape depending on the number of members in that family, and according to the bonds between them. For example, a family of a mother, a father and one child (let's suppose a daughter) has a triangular structure. In that triangle, there is—by nature—the special bond between the father and "daddy's little girl" that is like a covalent double bond in a chemical molecule. Between the mother and the daughter is a single bond, because it is not as special. Now, if the father and the mother are loyal and love each other, and the bond between them is strong, we'll say it's a double bond. If it's not as strong, that will make it a single bond. If the mother and father are divorced, then there is no bond between them, and if the relationship between them after divorce is antagonistic, then the forces between them are repelling forces. When the daughter reaches puberty and starts to move into adulthood, she is on a pathway to

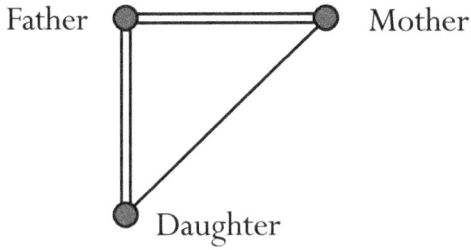

A FAMILY OF A LOVING FATHER & MOTHER & ONE DAUGHTER

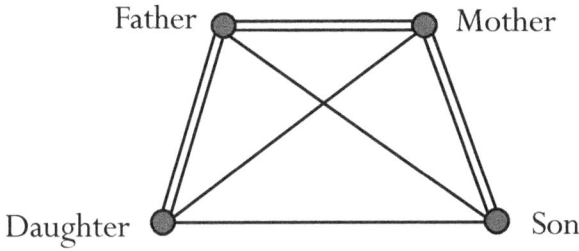

A FAMILY OF A LOVING FATHER, MOTHER, DAUGHTER & SON

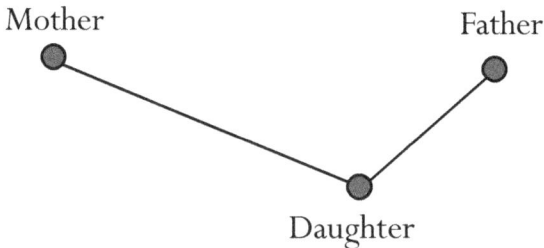

A FAMILY OF DIVORCED PARENTS WHERE
THE FATHER HAS REMARRIED

GEOMETRIC STRUCTURES OF THREE DIFFERENT FAMILIES.

define her own identity as a woman—separate from her mother's identity. The bond between the mother and the daughter starts to weaken, and the repelling forces begin to strengthen. If the mother and the father have a double bond between them, and the father and the daughter have a double bond between them, then the repelling forces between the mother and the daughter will stay tempered, and the geometric structure will have a better chance to retain its triangular shape. This will provide increased stability to the family, and give the daughter's transition into adulthood a better chance to be a more smooth process. If the father and the mother are divorced, the bond between them will not exist, the stable triangle will also not exist anymore, and the whole geometric structure of the family will weaken, making life more difficult. Now, let's suppose the father and the mother have an antagonistic relationship; the father will be hating on the mother, which becomes contagious to the daughter, thus strengthening the repelling forces between the mother and the daughter so much that the process might result in a complete disruption of that bond—which again leads to a more unstable life for everybody involved. I have seen this phenomenon happen so many times: where the mother and the daughter drift apart for many years to come only to have the daughter come back to see her mother when she is really ill or on her death bed, and become so riddled with guilt which cannot be shaken away.

I have seen the same phenomenon happen with boys and their fathers. The same exact scenario described above happens the same exact way, except this time, the double bond exists between the son and the mother (Oedipus Complex, anyone?), and after puberty, the son needs to find his own identity as a man separate from his father's. The same circumstances that might result in the total disruption of the bond between the son and his father occur, only to have the son come back after so many years of alienation when his father is very ill or dying, and become riddled with a great deal of hard-to-shake guilt. I know men usually don't cry at movies. Crying at movies is for girls, right? Except in one instance that doesn't fail to make most men cry. That happens when the story is about the difficult relationship between the father and the son, especially when the son has a chance to repent, or worse yet—when he decides to repent but doesn't get his chance to because of some unfortunate and uncontrollable twist of fate. I'm sure that you have seen men cry at movies then, haven't you? Well, that's just about the main reason that causes the majority of men to cry!

Then you might ask: why do these repelling forces between the father and the son and the mother and the daughter exist and lead to such heartbreak? Well, just imagine if these forces did not exist in nature. What will end up happening is that everybody who is born in a family remains content with their lot, and stays in that family and in the status quo. That can only go so far, because can you imagine what it will lead to if everybody stays that way generation upon generation? Stagnation! But that's not what happens in real life; the repelling forces cause the kids to get out and form their own families with their own different skills that will allow them to be able to tackle life in a different manner. That is meant to create variety, versatility, better adaptability and a better chance for the whole. Therefore, that process is evolutionary, but it becomes extremely more painful when everybody is coming from a broken family.

Teenagers need to understand that very well. They need to be smart and not act like brainless automatons fueled by hormones, and intoxicated by alcohol and drugs. They should not make their transition into adulthood more difficult on everybody including themselves by adding poisons to their rapidly evolving systems, and thus adding insult to injury! Keeping their system clean and exercising their mental capabilities is the only way they can be unique and navigate a treacherous environment. On the other hand, using alcohol and drugs is succumbing to "peer pressure" and "being a sheep." In the process of their stepping out into the real world, they should not be impolite or disrespectful because that does not require brainpower at all whatsoever. They have been given a brain for one reason only, and that is to use it.

In another scenario, when the father abandons the mother and the son for instance, the son puts the burden upon himself to make it up to his mother. That might lead to these forces consuming his whole life and he might become a "mama's boy." He becomes vulnerable to his mother's whims, and if that mother wants to keep him all to herself, he might never get married or have a successful relationship because she will always come first, thus making his life more difficult.

In a family of two, such as a mother and daughter or a father and son, the geometric structure is a linear one with a week bond—which means that if you're off at the beginning of the line by a small degree, the end of the line becomes very far from the intended destination. And, the weak bond will be very easy to break. That makes life very difficult for everybody and increases the likelihood of failure. The way to strengthen such a family is to create more bonds to strengthen the geometric structure with extended family members, and/or very close friends. The Collective Wisdom knew that it takes a village to raise a child.

But what would you do when some forces in the village are pulling your child in the wrong direction? And who doesn't know how powerful the outside forces like peer pressure are? What you can do is try to change these outside forces. You organize with the people like you and work hard toward the common good for all children, because that will be the only way to affect the peer pressure that is influencing your child. You save your child by saving all of humanity if you can. It is worth it, isn't it? That's what I am trying to do in this book.

These geometric structures of families I have described above are very simplistic ones, and often, family structures are a lot more complicated than this. Usually, there are more forces at play, but I tried to simplify the example as much as possible to make it clear. Other forces exist when there are other children involved, like sibling rivalry, for example. That serves to propel the children forward from very early on so they will get ahead. That also serves to temper the repelling forces between the father and sons, and mother and daughters, because the children will be competing for their parent's attention and approval.

The structure of a family with two children, e.g. one boy and one girl, will have different bonds forming multiple different triangles building a unique geometric structure like the triangulated polyhedron of a chemical molecule. There is the double bond between the son and the mother, the single bond between the son and the father and the bond between the father and the mother forming one triangle. Then, there is the double bond between the daughter and the father, the single bond between the daughter and the mother and the bond between the father and the mother forming another triangle. Then there is a bond between the son and the daughter, and a bond between the daughter and the mother, and a double bond between the son and the mother forming a third triangle; and so on and so forth... Again, the final geometric structure depends on what kind of relationship exists between the father and the mother. It can be a double bond or a single bond or no bond at all, etc. In each instance the geometric structure created has a different shape, which affects the outcome.

In summary, each family is different because of the number of people who constitute that family and the kind of bonds between them—its own unique and separate organism. So, if there are more than just two kids in the family, the dynamics change again. This will sound paradoxical, but it might make it easier on you to have more children. An old proverb says, "The mother of 10,

God helps her; the mother of one, God help her!" That might be because the most difficult thing to do is to keep an only child entertained, which is a problem that does not exist when you have 10 children. And often, problems arise out of boredom. It also might be because "there is strength in numbers," and that strength will protect against the bad forces generated by peer pressure.

That again is simplifying the picture too much, because in a family, there are other forces at play. For example, the family can be poor, and that will create financial stress, or rich, which will not create financial stress. There might be another family member affecting its structure, let's say a mother-in-law that can be nosy, which will cause stress. The kind of bond between the mother-in-law and her child will affect the bond between the father and the mother, and she will have bonds with the kids, which can have varying strengths and can be of substantial impact on the family.

I am sure you have already noticed the special bonding that happens between grandparents and grandchildren. Somebody made a joke about it and said that grandparents and grandchildren love each other so much because they have the same enemy–the parents! Ha-ha. But the meaning of this joke is quite valuable because as you can remember, popular jokes point to the patterns that operate in the real world. The Universal Subconscious has realized that there is a special bond that exists between grandparents and grandchildren, and, there is a good chance you had a special relationship with your grandparents, if you had one that you can remember. I'm also sure you will remember that you did not see your grandparents (and no other child sees their grandparents) as these ugly, wrinkled, shriveled-up old people that smell like old people! No, you don't see them that way. You see them as beautiful, and you love them and have a special connection to them. Those forces could be tapped into for the benefit of our children: a teenage girl who is in the process of separating from her mother will likely have more ears for her grandmother, and similarly, a teenage boy will have more ears for his grandfather. When we realize how these dynamics work, we can use them to our advantage. So, instead of parking our parents in a retirement facility somewhere, we can keep them close, and utilize the strength of their bond with our children to make our lives easier and more successful, because the village starts with the extended family.

That brings us to the more compound family where there might have been a divorce between the father and the mother, and one or both of the parents have remarried, which will add a stepparent to the equation. When the father and the mother divorce, first of all, that will create financial stress. Second, they would still have to deal with each other for the sake of the kids. Third, the son gets especially angry with his father, and the daughter gets especially angry with her mother. The son becomes his mother's protector, and will start having problems with her when she brings another man into her life, especially if that new man is mean to him. The daughter becomes her father's protector and the same thing happens to her when her father remarries. On the other hand, the

stepfather or the stepmother will not have a strong blood
bond to the stepchildren and will often have a conflict of
interest with them, especially if they have children of their
own. Their bonds to their own children are going to be
stronger than their bonds to their stepchildren, and their
interest is going to be vested in their own children even
at the expense of their stepchildren. These dynamics lead
to the weakening of the bonds in the new family and to an
unstable geometric structure, thus making it very hard to
maintain. It will take a major force to be able to pull all of
this together and make it work. And where will that force
come from? In the majority of cases, it is simply not there.
So that brings up the question: how does divorce help any
if it leads to the situation described above? If the father or
mother had thought that divorce was going to make their
lives better, they need to think again, because divorce
only complicates matters and leads to weakening of the
family structure and more problems. So if the problems
of marriage in a simple family were difficult to bear, how
does adding to these problems in a complicated family
as described above make life any easier? In most cases
it doesn't. That is why you see that the divorcing party
frequently ends up divorcing again, only to make life even
more miserable and complicated for themselves. In the
end, they give up and settle, not because they are finally
happy but because they are tired or run out of money,
which means there is no more force.

Now, I'm not trying to say that there should not be
a place for divorce in a marriage with children, because
there is a place for divorce under the circumstances where

the marriage is detrimental to one's health or life. When that is the case, then the price to pay by complicating life more will be worth it. It becomes a question of risk vs. reward ratio. You will be willing to pay a heftier price with a more complicated family because you would be risking your health or your life if you didn't.

But in our day and age, a lot of people have been taking a very big risk and complicating their lives for the wrong reasons. Some couples have been divorcing because they think that if they change a difficult spouse, their lives will get better—but they are short sited, and ignorant of the dynamics that result from a move like that, which will end up complicating their lives even further, and making it more difficult for them. So, people need to do their math correctly before they divorce. And what about the one that marries somebody who was divorced before? How can they guarantee that such a person who might have run away from the problems in a marriage before them, or caused their spouse to run away, will not run away from the problems in a marriage with them, or cause them to run away? Because a lot of times, when everybody's lives become so complicated in a situation like this, the risk of failure grows. Again, as I said before, that explains the serial divorces that have become more and more common.

And then you might say that you are looking for your soulmate, and if you find "the one," your life will improve. Does such a thing really exist? Yes it might exist, but it's such a very rare occurrence that it becomes the subject of books and movies. Soulmates are very rare because if they were not, how could we explain the amount of intimate relationships that a human being has in a free society before he/she finally settles down to get married? I'll explain it this way: I have a relationship with someone I think is my soulmate, but he leaves me because he doesn't think I'm his soulmate, so the relationship fails. But your soulmate is not your one predestined match if you're not their soul "mate" at the same time! So the fact that you thought that person was 'the one" was a mistake and that situation did not exist the way you had thought. That's why I said it is rare. That also explains the big number of successful arranged marriages! A lot of arranged marriages succeed because the parties involved have the same interest, which is to get married and form a family, so they declare their intentions to marry immediately, and they work together towards the same goals. That improves the odds for success of their transaction.

SEX

Here, I am not going to tell you anything you haven't heard many times before: and it might be because of their biological clock, but from early on, women are more inclined by nature to want to have children and families. A big part of the effort they exert in life is to get a husband and a father for their children, and to make a home. A girl can be very smart and outgoing and good at science and math, etc. until she hits puberty and she has to heed the call of nature. She changes and a lot of her attention shifts. This force of nature caused by a small quantity of a chemical hormone is extremely strong and extremely hard to resist, and it takes unbelievable mental effort and sacrifice to be able to exert some control over it. The girl does not become less smart as a result of that. No! She just becomes a "mother-in-waiting." On the other hand, when the boys hit puberty and testosterone starts circulating in their system, their interest turns to making money. They become "providers-in-waiting." Testosterone can also fuel violence in the pursuit of financial gain, and that ends up populating prisons and wars with men.

Then sex happens, and that is where all of the dynamics can go wrong, and do go wrong especially in a free society. That is because what not too many people understand is that sex is a commodity. I know, I know, this statement is going to generate a big loud scream of NO!!! Not true!!!

But in reality, take a moment and think about it before you react—that statement is true. Sex is a commodity. Because you cannot deny that sex has nothing to do with romantic love, especially when it comes to non-committed men. We know that women want relationships and non-committed men want sex. For these men, sex is a goal. For women, sex is not the endgame by itself, but a means to an end, which is building a family. Giving sex is always for something in return. As a result, there is always a price for sex. Women in Liberia knew that, so in 2003 they collectively withheld the sex and their country was able to achieve peace after 14 years of civil war. Sex is a commodity and has monetary value. Some men pay prostitutes even though they can sleep with a regular girl for free, and that is because they cannot afford what's free. There is more expected out of that "free" relationship. Those men know it and they do not want to give more. Sex without commitment is cheaper. Women hate prostitutes because they lower the price of sex. I wouldn't be surprised if it wasn't the women who influenced men to make prostitution illegal. Just watch when young girls start labeling each other a "slut" and telling boys who is a "slut" and who is not. By age six! And you know who ends up being a "slut?" The one who is more "free" with her behavior!

The old civilizations realized that dynamic and have been trying to control sex in an attempt to improve society by minimizing out-of-wedlock births, which are a financial burden onto society, and trying to minimize the emotional and physical illnesses that result from lack of commitment. That's why you see that most of these old civilizations have put restrictions on the sex market by restricting the girls from very early on in their lives. The man had to pay first before getting it. That man had to pay with commitment, or with commitment and money. That way, the women would be protected, because as you can remember, women's end goal is not sex. But in these societies, a major force has to be generated to restrain the girls and counteract the effect of nature on them. A lot of times, that force ends up causing emotional and physical harm to the same girls that had to be protected in the first place: this force can reach a tragic point when the girls' sexuality before marriage is punishable by death in the appalling practice of "honor killing," by their own families, i.e. for the sake of the perpetrator's honor and reputation in society. Yes, that's true! For the sake of his status, the perpetrator spills his own blood! Such a cowardly act! People in these societies need to understand that.

You can also see, for example, that the Hasidic Jews, the traditional Christians and Moslems require their women to cover up and they prohibit out of wedlock sex. Restricting the sex market that way improves the value of sex and women. Men will do anything to get it, even if they have to commit in marriage. Marriage makes women happy because they can achieve their goals easier this way. With marriage, the man has a better chance to get more steady sex, the woman has a better chance to form a family, and everybody has a better chance to be more fulfilled. Women understand how this dynamic works. That's why most of the women that cover up do it because they want to, because they realize the amount of power that it gives them in the equation of sex. If you don't agree, ask them; they will tell you they are happy that "the other women are covered up also" because it limits their husband's temptation and choices. Let's ask ourselves this question: if all of the women in Afghanistan decided to shed the burqa at the same time, who would be able to stop them? A man might be able to stop his wife, but he cannot stop his mother, and if he can, the other men can't.

Thus, restricting sex before marriage ought to result in decreasing the ills of society—although that road is fraught with the danger of loss of life to whoever errs. And of course, there would still be a lot of problems after marriage happens. So is that the only way to restrict sex before marriage, or could we find a better way? This is what I know: all girls should come to realize that sex should not be free, and collectively withhold it until marriage. Sex has a sublime value, and that value has to be implemented.

Also, sex is like food. When there is hunger, it becomes more valuable. When there is gluttony and people are not hungry anymore, the food is not very good and it leads to illness. Sexual hunger serves in the equation like pain: "No pain, no gain." It gives enough oomph to achieve great things like building a family. Therefore, keep the hunger. Without it, a lot of the men won't need to commit, and they don't.

On the other hand, once you start becoming sexually active, you will need to have sex routinely in a balanced fashion for better health—like nutrition. Hopefully that will happen in a committed relationship because access will be more difficult otherwise.

When sex is withheld or prohibited for one reason or another, its price becomes very hefty and it can even cost some people's lives. Look at the great love stories of all time: one of the most important variables present in their equations is the strength of the obstacle preventing the relationship from happening. The best example is in the story of *Romeo and Juliet* where the lovers were prohibited from freely consummating their love to their heart's desire. Without that force, the love story wouldn't have been that great.

LOVE

That brings us to the subject of Cinderella and the prince, or Sleeping Beauty and the prince. What a hoax is being pulled off on young girls all over the world! To make a young girl of any means believe that she might have a good chance at getting a prince even if she is a pauper is such a lie and a crime. "Why?" you might ask. It's because princes and rich people are generally not allowed to marry beneath them. Their families will do everything in their power to prevent such a marriage from happening because the poor one is considered to be a gold-digger. This is true even for Cinderella and Sleeping Beauty: their fathers were rich already! Yes, it's true that they were deprived of their father's riches, but that was just a temporary condition that could have been easily resolved in court!

So for all of those young girls out there, your chance at getting a real prince or a rich man is close to nil. It happens so rarely that it makes for a great subject in movies because it is nearly fictional. It happens only when the benefit outweighs the risk, or when the parents lose control over their son because he has grown to be so jaded by their riches, or when the son disavows his parents and their riches to marry whomever he wants to. So girls wake up! Marry a good guy and make him your prince—it's only the good guy who will make you his princess. Look at

Princess Diana: Prince Charles married her, but Camilla was the real princess of his heart. And if you can't find the guy to make you his princess, then make yourself one: learn how to cook gourmet meals for yourself and your family, learn how to create beautiful things in your world using your hands and brain and intelligence. If you can't afford something, try to make it if possible. The same thing applies for the guys: nobody will make a guy feel like a king other than his loving family. When I was little, my father was just a regular government employee, but to me, he was the greatest man ever created!

I'm addressing this subject because I have noticed that people are not marrying as much anymore! I have also noticed that finances have a lot to do with it. Problems arise whenever a marrying party is more fortunate than the other one, especially when the difference of their riches is large. How could the richer one guarantee that the other party is not after them for their money? They can't! And if finances are not in the picture now because the two parties are so much in love, they become a major issue later when love gets tempered. That's why the term gold-digger has been wielded to describe the less fortunate, and that is usually the woman because of what I will explain later. The solution to that uncertainty is for everybody to have pre-nuptial agreements even if they are not rich. Some older societies have realized these dynamics and implemented pre-nuptial agreements as the basis for all marriages.

This brings us to the question: What is love? Love is a force that binds people together.

Understanding that love is a binding force helps to explain the various notions that have been put out there by the Collective Subconscious when it comes to dealing with the nuances of relationships. An example is when people say, "I love you, but I don't like you." It's such an ambiguous phrase and yet when you translate it, it makes perfect sense. What that phrase means is that I don't like you, but I still have a bond with you/I'm still bound to you. Another very ambiguous notion that has intrigued individuals in romantic relationships or marriage is when they are told that the relationship has to end because the other party "likes them, but does not love them!" Such a puzzling notion, and yet its meaning is perfectly simple and clear. What it means is that the other party likes them, but does not have a bond with them, or does not feel bound to them. In this case, the ideal thing to do is to just move on.

What the above also means is that liking somebody does not exist on the same spectrum as love. Love has its own spectrum from the weakest to the strongest, and "lust," "crushes," "romantic love," "love" and "dependency" all belong on that spectrum, with lust and dependency being on the opposite ends from each other.

When we understand that fact well, we can't help but pity teenagers and young adults of this day and age. Because when they used to have "crushes" and "love" and "relationships," now they have been brainwashed into settling for "like," "like like," and "friends with benefits" instead!!! That's the best they can hope for and get in their young years–when they are the most beautiful, full of stamina and energy and vigor and love of life and brightness and happiness and good intentions and naiveté and good heartedness—NO BONDING! No wonder our teenagers and young adults are getting so messed up. A big number of them are acting out, becoming very difficult to deal with and resorting to bonding with drugs and alcohol instead! No wonder!

As I have just made it very clear, understanding once and for all that love is a binding force helps shed light on the dynamics of human relationships. For example, what causes a person who was bound to you to lose that bond and lose the love could be a multitude of reasons, but in most instances, it involves an opposing, more powerful force that creates stronger bonds with somebody else and/ or with something else (i.e. a romantic relationship with another person, a relationship with alcohol or drugs, or both).

The binding force of love can vary in strength and duration from person to person. That's what creates imbalance in the relationships, and leads people to give love different derogatory names like "dependency" and "lust," and has led to the confusing picture of love.

Lust is a very short-lived love condition, and what is dependency if it is not very strong love? Dependency happens when your love is so strong—when you feel bound to a person to the point where you depend on being with that person like you depend on your arm or eyes. That person's love for you might not be as strong; he or she will not be able to understand your feelings, and your feelings might annoy them because they don't bind to you to the same degree. On the other hand, it's a dangerous predicament to be in, because what would happen if that person were not there for you anymore? It could actually cost you your life. We witness that phenomenon sometimes when one spouse dies right after the other one. Now ideally, the best structure between two people who love each other is created when they are both on the "same wavelength," and feel the same way towards each other, because that harmony will generate a greater force, giving them more power to be able to tackle the difficulties of life.

Romantic love and lust are the forces that bring people together physically, because without these forces, who would ever want to mix their juices with anybody else's, and get exposed to all kinds of foreign germs, attitudes and behaviors?

A non-committed man is the one who wants to bind to you for sex only, and will stay with you as long as his lust lasts, and he will not change his mind even if you provide him with the ideal relationship. That man's endgame is fulfilled when he's done having sex with you. But since a woman's endgame is not sex, the prostitute and call girl achieves her goal when she gets paid for it, and the other woman will "stay bound" to the person she has sex with, because she still needs to achieve her goal, which is to have a family and kids. Men know very well what I'm talking about, and they say that the woman "catches feelings" for them! Ha-ha! I can't help but laugh in sarcasm at how ironic and cruel that mental picture is! She catches feelings the same way you catch a disease! And in reality, that situation she finds herself in is akin to a diseased state. She suffers from an affliction that has no cure, when she stays bound to somebody after lust is fulfilled! I told you the Collective Subconscious is very smart! This is the situation where many women become jaded and decide that they too can have commitment-free sex in an effort to prove to themselves and others that they are strong.

Women need to understand that dynamic very well. You need to know that nature intended for you to "catch feelings" for the guy, and thus you get in a state that could jeopardize your health. So don't put yourself in that losing position, and get in a relationship with a non-committed man. You should avoid that predicament and have sex with a committed man only, because it's only the committed man who will care for your feelings once you "catch them."

Therefore, when you meet a suitor, don't give him sex first and then find out if he's committed or not. Have him commit first, and then give him sex, otherwise your chance of failure will be great. I'm sure a lot of women recognize what I'm talking about: we meet somebody who might be so-so, we have sex with him and find ourselves getting stuck on him for some mysterious reason! Isn't it? That explains why sex and romantic love go together hand-in-hand for the woman. It will take a very jaded woman who has had severe negative feedback from relationships gone wrong, or a woman messed up on alcohol and/or drugs, before she will start to be able to work on stopping her emotions right after lust is fulfilled while that does not require any significant effort from the non-committed man. Once that man is done having sex with you, it clears up his mind; he drops you to pursue his advancement in life with another woman who will help him achieve a better status, while you might stay stuck on him for a while, which will make your life very difficult, especially if you end up having kids from that relationship.

Because of the dynamics I have described above, life seems to be more difficult for the woman. But these vagabond men are not aware that their bad behavior will impact them in the future, because sooner or later they will "reap what they sow." When their main goal is to screw, they will get screwed. When they don't help the woman make a family, she will not make a home for them; and when they plant their seed and run away, they will have no claim to the harvest. One of these days they will lose their vigor, and when that happens, they will not find one shoulder to lean on.

Life is very difficult. It is difficult to stay balanced, and people need strength. That strength comes from bonding–from love. Individuals alone are too weak by themselves, which is why they form families, organizations and groups. A person alone is like a stick that can be broken with a snap. Put two sticks together and it becomes harder to break them. Put three sticks together and you end up creating a triangular cross-sectional shape that is even more difficult to snap. And who does not know the proverb that says, "Divide and conquer?" Because when you divide, you weaken the structure.

Achieving the balance is very important–not tipping the scale in one direction or the other. Looking at the widely accepted bell curve, we can see that if you go to one extreme or the other, you go down. Everybody tells you to do things in moderation. Too much love becomes dependency, too much ambition becomes greed, while on the other hand, too little ambition is complacency, and too little love is lust. Everything at the wrong concentration becomes a poison, "too much of a good thing is bad thing," and everything that increases decreases. We have to keep the balance. It is so easy for us to overdo it, and err, especially when we lose our moral grounds. We should stay humble, and never become arrogant. We have to accept a little happiness and be more content. We also ought to find balanced love and avoid settling into lust or dependency.

DESTINY AND CHOICE

But then you might ask: if set natural forces dictate patterns of behavior, does that mean that everything is predetermined? Or do we still have a choice?

The answer is not either/or; the answer is both. Things appear to be predetermined, but yes we do have a choice, and our choice does make a difference.

Let me explain to you how this equation works, because the Collective Subconscious got it right–it is an equation. The variables in the equation interact with each other and give an outcome. Some of these variables are the things we decide–our decisions–and they affect the end result. If the other variables are what they are, and we cannot change them, we still end up changing the outcome of the equation by what we decide to do, or not to do– because deciding to not do something is still something we did. This is how our choice affects the outcome.

People who have to chose try to make a "well-informed decision" and know to "weigh the options" by looking at the "pros and cons." They can be "calculating" and "do their math right." So why do we often feel that we made the best decision but the outcome was unexpected and that it was predetermined? Also, is there a way to make smarter decisions?

It is the act of deciding that makes us believe that the outcome of our actions depends on our choices. But in reality, the results depend on the equation that includes our choices plus the other variables. We might know some of these variables, and some might not be known to us. The more of these variables that we know, the more control we feel that we have over the outcome. It is the unknown variables that make us feel that we have no control, and that God has actually dictated the outcome—that the outcome was predetermined and that it was our "destiny." To make a better choice that will allow us to predict the outcome with better accuracy, we need to become better educated and informed about the variables involved in the equation. If it is not possible to know all the variables, then all the possible different outcomes need to be figured out with different degrees of probability.

For example, I buy a house with a 30-year mortgage. Because of the job I have, my calculations tell me that I can afford to pay for the house and stay in it as long as I need to. The variable I didn't know about when I bought the house was that the company I'm working for is about to collapse, and it will be out of business in a year. That means I will be out of a job soon. After a year, I cannot afford my house anymore, and I have to find another job, which might necessitate moving away. This demonstrates how I had a choice to formulate a plan for my life, but my destiny and "God" had something different for my future. It's only a matter of lack of knowledge. And looking back at it, after a year passes by and all of the variables become known, I understand what transpired. But were my calculations done correctly in the first place when I bought the house? Should I have thought about the possibility of the company going out of business? What about considering whether my health was going to serve me long enough to work and pay for 30 years? All these possibilities are variables that I needed to factor into the equation that would have guided me in making a more informed decision about buying the house, and to formulate an alternative plan if necessary.

The same process works the same way at the scale of larger operations of companies and countries. For example, the outcome will surprise us when we do not know about some fraudulent actions, because of lack of oversight over an organization. Why do we need to have oversight over an organization you might ask? It's because greed should always be factored into a financial equation. Because the force of greed exists, we need to have the government police not only the individuals, but also the companies.

We usually make our decisions based on the variables we know, and what kind of person we are: what our personality is like, or what our temperament is at that moment. Does it mean then that when I make a choice, my decision has been dictated by certain predetermined factors, like my personality and temperament? Only if we let it be. As I explained earlier, we can control our temperament with our thoughts, and we should. Therefore, in reality, we ought to be capable of making free choices. That explains how, for example, some hard-core addicts can turn their lives around—and I'm talking about all addicts: drug addicts, addicts to food, sex addicts and addicts to bad behavior.

When we make an informed decision in good conscience using our full mental capabilities, we should never regret it whatever the outcome might be. Because when we made that decision at that time, we factored the variables we knew into the equation, and we made the best judgment possible under those circumstances, using a sane mind. After the outcome is clear, becoming aware of the unknown variables should not cause us to regret our decisions. Once we have made our conscientious, courageous choices, we should live with the consequences courageously. On the other hand, if our mind was under the influence of drugs and alcohol, then we should regret our bad decisions.

Sometimes, we make decisions based on the variables we know, and the outcome is better than we expected due to the variables that we didn't know. At other times, the outcome can be worse. When unexpected outcomes happen, we look back, and realize the existence of those variables that were at play that were previously unknown to us, and then we understand. We appreciate in hindsight, and we say, "Hindsight is 20/20."

When we make decisions that end up having an unpleasant outcome, we feel as if we're being punished. If the outcome is totally unplanned for, our whole life gets steered out of our control, and we end up having to follow a different path in our life. At that time, when we realize how we couldn't prevent something from happening, we feel that it was predetermined, and that it "had" to happen. And we can't help but believe that the outcome was the actual reason for what transpired.

THE REASON IS THE OUTCOME.

THE CONSCIOUS AND
THE SUBCONSCIOUS

We use our conscious level of thinking to accumulate enough knowledge and information to include in the equations that we are trying to solve. But we should not forget to tap into our subconscious because it is very smart. When we rely on our conscious level of thinking without tapping into our subconscious, we can get brainwashed very easily by words and by other people's ideas, and can be led down a certain pathway that is not necessarily best for us.

Your brain has a lot of knowledge and power in it, as well as problem solving capabilities. Words have been distracting your conscious mind. Tune into your subconscious because it knows exactly what's good for you. I'm sure you've experienced how it works before. Haven't you had a time when you were leaving your home, for example, and something kept nagging at you and telling you that you forgot something inside? You don't listen and go on with your day only to remember later what you had forgotten! Another example is when you have a dilemma you're pondering. You think about it at night before going to sleep. When you wake up the next day, you have the answer as either a clear thought or as a strong "gut feeling." That's because your conscious brain sleeps, but your subconscious doesn't. It's working throughout the night healing your body, helping restore your tissues to their original memory, and doing the math for you to solve your problem. That's why you wake up refreshed in the morning. Of course that mechanism gets disrupted in a diseased state, or when you have chemicals on board that interfere with the normal functions of the brain like alcohol, sleeping pills or a multitude of other drugs.

Our subconscious thinking is very smart, and operates with intelligent automation following certain innate dictates. To become aware of that fact, we just have to stop and listen and bring that information up to our conscious level. Then we can add it to our conscious knowledge to figure out the equation at hand. When we do that, we will all hear what our subconscious is telling us, and we will be smarter for it. I have already given multiple examples throughout this book that attest to how smart the Collective Subconscious is, bringing that knowledge up to the conscious level for you. I'm not telling you anything you didn't know before; I'm just shining a bright new light on it.

So how come people do not stop and listen all of the time? It's because it is not efficient. There are hundreds of decisions that need to be made each day, and there is no need to ponder each one of them, otherwise life will come to a stop. To keep doing calculations constantly is exhausting to the mind, crippling and unnecessary. What people usually do, the way the system is set up, is to act impulsively either as the effect of being brainwashed or based off of their instinct. Acting instinctively is directed

by the subconscious. The subconscious is factoring in
the most important variables that carry the most weight
without needing to factor in every variable, thus coming
out with the best answers. Because it is the variables with
the most weight that usually affect the outcome the most,
the majority of time this method works without problems
because inherently, the system is attuned to the fact
that the outcome possibilities are limited. For example,
"Boy meets Girl and they like each other"… what could
the outcome be? Two things only: 1) Boy and Girl stay
together or 2) Boy and Girl don't stay together.

Usually, the subconscious thinking is brought up to
the conscious level and analyzed in the case of heightened
awareness, like during the formulation of specific plans
of action in the case of major events affecting individuals,
companies or countries—or in crises. When that happens, it
is referred to as "awakening."

The best attestation to the intelligence of the
subconscious is the fact that even what's called "instinctual
impulsivity" can be advantageous to the human race.
That impulsivity happens when we don't include all of
the variables in the equation, and the subconscious ends
up causing us to act instinctively based on the strongest
forces involved. Take for example the fact that nowadays,
more than 40 % of children are born to unwed mothers.
The majority of people would say that this is the result of
impulsivity on the mother's part because her decisions will
lead to a difficult life for herself and the child. But is that
really a bad thing? Let's look at it this way: if these mothers
were not impulsive and did not have these kids, it would

have meant that 40% of the children wouldn't have been born. And what would have that meant for our country? If these unwed mothers were not impulsive to their own detriment and suffering year after year, wouldn't that then eventually lead to the extinction of our new generations? I certainly believe it would.

So, this demonstrates how the subconscious is trying to save us. But then you might ask: why is the subconscious failing to make life better for the mother? The answer might be that there is nothing more fulfilling to a "mother-in-waiting' than to have a child, even at the cost of suffering… because everybody knows that birth control is readily available, and then don't forget that even though these mothers might have gotten pregnant by mistake, they still had the chance to abort the child if the forces were not strong enough to make them keep it.

That leads us to the conscious level of thinking. Between the conscious and the subconscious, our brain is equipped with the tools needed to figure it all out. The scientist's brain is not better than yours. First of all, the scientists did not invent their brains. All normal brains, and even some brains that were not born normal, are equipped with a lot of potential in them, as we see when examining the brains of the idiot savants, the autistic, and those with Attention Deficit Disorder (ADD). The scientists' brains put information together and make sense of it, and then they relay it to us. That information in turn has to make sense to us also, before we will be able to learn it and delegate it to our memory. That does not make our brains less capable than those of the scientists, but all the other

variables in their lives, other than just their brain, have
come together to lead them to make their discoveries. We
could have made those same discoveries ourselves if the
variables were right for us. But that does not mean that
we should minimize what they have achieved, because the
variables that are part of the equation that lead them to
their discoveries often include aloneness, pain, suffering and
sacrifice. In other words, they pay a price, and we don't.
On the other hand, for the inquiring mind, there is always
room for more discoveries. Scientists have not solved all the
problems. For example, hearing-aid technology is lacking
and is not serving the elderly needs well. Similarly, vision
correction technology, airplane technology and safety
need improvement, and we haven't conquered obesity and
cancer. To the contrary, the rate of obese people and those
diagnosed with cancer has been on the rise...

Therefore, the brain of the expert is not better than
yours. The brain of the boys is not better at science and
math than the brain of the girls. The difference between
your brain and that of the "experts," between a boy's brain
and a girl's brain, is interest. When you become interested
in what the experts are interested in, or in science and
math, and you decide to study it, you learn it. Somebody
who has a lot of physical power and energy in his/her
body will find it hard to sit down long enough to study
to become an academic expert, but that does not mean
that they lack the power in their brain to develop mental
expertise of a sport they can master. It just means that
their equation is different because it includes a significant
amount of physical power, that's all.

WOMEN AND MEN

That leads us to the question: Why are so many women that way, having children out of wedlock and jeopardizing their future and the future of their children? And what happened to the men? Why don't they stick around and take care of their women and children?

Women and men start life on somewhat of an equal footing as children, and then hormones happen. When hormones set in, that fuel drives the women to make families, and drives the men to become providers. It immediately puts women at an economic disadvantage, and creates the monetary disparities between the sexes, which is a sad state of affairs because society now is forcing everybody to rely on themselves financially. Some women are able to avert that fate with extreme determination and willpower from very early on, which is great. Sometimes though, it is at the expense of having future families and children because the longer a woman delays childbearing, the less her chances. A lot of other women become major achievers in society again after they raise their child, while the rest of the women will remain dependant financially on the man or on society.

But unfortunately, society has convinced men that they ought not support a woman, or that a woman who needs financial support is a gold digger. If you follow that route, you will end up having individuals that have to be financially independent from each other, which makes them weaker. On the downside, you will find many girls who have fought against the very strong power of nature and failed, and boys who are working toward a career with no clear destination of anybody to provide for. You end up having a bunch of very depressed teenagers and young adults with a futile ultimate goal in mind: support yourself and be alone! (Divide and conquer!) If we want to help improve their lives, we have to help them set the goal that nature intended. It is possible and admirable to be able to have a good marriage between career and family. There is also nothing wrong with a woman being a housewife. The work a housewife does in the home has been estimated to be worth over 100,000 dollars per year. Some people contest that figure, but actually, a woman's work at home is priceless. A woman is a psychologist, chief operating officer, accountant, cook, housekeeper, driver, teacher, etc.

For some men I would say this: Don't do what "Borat" did and seek a "Pamela Anderson" when your salvation could be the girl right next-door to you! Don't perpetuate the bad deeds that your father has done to your mother. A girl is no "bitch" and no "hoe!" A girl is what has become your mother! Take care of women. They may be weaker physically but can have a big "muscle" in their brain: the brain is like a muscle because when you exercise it, it gets stronger. Benefit from their brain. Respect their point of view. They see things from a different perspective; they tend to be long-term planners and see things more clearly into the future. This trait adds knowledge. Men are faster decision-makers, and usually have more strength. Women have more endurance.

What men don't understand is that if they have a family with a wife and children they will become "king" of the roost. Other than his parents, nobody will ever love a man more than his children, and his wife if they are on the same wavelength. He doesn't have to be rich at all. He just needs to provide within his means, and he will be king. To his children, he will be more than adequate, especially to his daughters. What has been happening instead is that some men plant their seed and run away, and they end up being hated by the women and children they abandon–also they still might not achieve their economic goals. So they end up losing on all fronts, and they suffer. We also end up having women that suffer and children that suffer. Men and women will be forced to have multiple partners and more children with them, which will cause life to become more complicated for everybody, and will lead to financial stress, an increased risk of failure, and to emotional and physical disease. The whole society will have to carry the economic burden that ensues, and society suffers.

Society has been encouraging women to become financially independent and lessen the impact the absence of a male partner will have on them and their children. Some women thus "empowered" have concluded that there is no need for a man in their lives. This has raised a serious question in their minds and in the minds of men about what the real value of a man is for a family and for society. "Man" is not just a poking, STD gathering and transmitting machine. "Man" is not just a sperm donor. "Man" is not just a provider. "Man" forms stable families because "Man" creates bonds with the spouse and the children that result in a more stable geometric structure that is harder to disrupt. "Man" is essential for raising well-balanced children, especially self-respecting girls, and to give a good example to the boys. The absence of a man from families has created many ills in society. To the good man who understands what I'm talking about, and who wants to do the right thing, I would say this: You've been belittled and minusculed enough! Step up to the plate and hold your head up high because you have a sublime, irreplaceable role in life to play!

Our society has been sick. A lot of women are staying pathologically bitter at their mothers because their fathers did not stay with them. A lot of men are staying pathologically bitter at their fathers because they did not stay with their mothers, and that's because a lot of fathers don't stick around to temper those pathological feelings, and contribute to the mental wellbeing of their children. Don't get rid of your spouse to make your life easier now, because it will make it harder on you in the future when your kids are growing. Giving children toys and gadgets and material things creates spoiled, destructive brats. What children need more than anything is a father and a mother and a stable geometric structure in the home.

Second, a large number of people of all ages have been resorting to prescription narcotics or street drugs or alcohol to numb their feelings instead of solving their problems. These chemicals numb the brain and widen the emotional distance between people, which creates more problems. You add emotional distance to physical distance and the outcome you get is a bunch of lonely, weak, vulnerable, miserable individuals.

On the other hand, the rate of obesity and cancer has been increasing. Instead of preventing cancer, we're being told that we can live with it as a chronic disease now! How reassuring! A collaborative reanalysis of data from 51 epidemiological studies of women with breast cancer published in The Lancet in 1997 showed that *there is a statistically significant increase in breast cancer risk among users of any hormone replacement therapy that increased with increased duration of hormone use.* Therefore, hormones from birth control meds have been CAUSING an epidemic of breast cancer, and amongst other things, leading to the mutilation of a large number of women's breasts. One out of eight women will develop breast cancer during her lifetime. A man who is in harmony with you will help you achieve birth control without making you endanger your life for it. Then, as women age, and even before they hit menopause, their fertility declines to the point where a large number of them cannot get pregnant anymore, and not even with fertility treatments! When men age, they still might be able to father children, but their equipment gradually loses potency to the point where a large number of them become totally impotent—the decline in erectile function for every decade increase in age is 12%.

Lack of commitment has also lead to promiscuity that has lead to an explosion of STDs. STDs are infecting a large number of the sexually active, and leading to the mutilation of sexual organs. Also, a quarter of males living a western lifestyle develop symptomatic enlargement of the prostate by age 50, half of them by age 60 to 70, and 90 percent of them by age 90. The National Cancer Institute reports that prostate cancer is the most commonly diagnosed cancer among men in the United States, and that the incidence rates for clinical prostate cancer in western men are 30 to 50 times higher than those for Asian men, while the incidence for African American men is 200 times higher. Every year, there are approximately 200,000 newly diagnosed cases of prostate cancer in men age 55 and above. That means there are about four million six hundred thousand cases between the ages of 55 and 78! And if that's not an epidemic, then I don't really know what is! Therefore, as western men age, a large number of them develop significant problems with their equipment, and they develop a condition I call "Floppy Disc Syndrome"—when their flag stands at half-mast in mourning! Then they turn into these bald, potbellied, impotent, incontinent guys who slowly lose function and have nobody to stand by them because they stood by nobody in the past!

PEER PRESSURE

Now what about those forces in society that make the majority of people feel inadequate? In this free market world, businesses and corporations drive society. They can afford to use the media for reach, to make their ideas influential by repeatedly advertising to sell their fare. The only way they can persuade you to buy their product is to convince you that your life is lacking something without it, and they use peer pressure to manipulate you. They play on your weaknesses, your insecurity. They use the forces of your envy and greed against you. That's where the feeling of "lacking" and "inadequacy" comes from, only if you let it.

Another cause is when the media shows you that your virtual neighbors are doing better than you. Your virtual neighbors are the ones you see on the screen like the stars, and athletes, etc. When you socialize with your real neighbors and you find out that they are more like you, you feel more adequate. Your real neighbors most probably have a similar socio-economic status to yours. If they are doing better than you financially, you might have a good chance to work a little harder and measure up. But when you don't socialize with your neighbors, and you spend too much time with the TV, then you will constantly feel inadequate with a very slim chance to ever being able to catch up, and you might feel constantly poor, even when you're not.

You want to feel rich right away? Don't forget that "the richest man, whate'er his lot, is the one content with what he's got." Therefore, stop comparing your life to what you see on TV. Instead of doing that, look at the real poor people of the world, and count your blessings, because it's only then that you will realize how fortunate you really are, and how much potential you actually have.

For instance, I know a lot of guys whose goal in life is to get a "crib" like the ones they see on MTV. Why won't they feel adequate with a small, clean one-bedroom apartment and a loving family?? Envy, that's why! Envy is that force of nature that is being used against you, but it cannot be used against you if you are aware and you don't let it happen.

Men want to feel adequate before starting a family. The forces in society these days try to make everybody feel inadequate. They are not strong enough to counteract the natural forces driving the women to have babies, but they stop the men from wanting to have families until they are well established in life. That might happen later on, and it might not happen at all. It depends on the amount of ambition they have, because it is ok for them to have ambition, but it is not ok to have greed. The women need to be satisfied with less material things also. Won't that be better than being a single mother with no financial support or male support? Why wouldn't the men and women start small, be on the same wavelength, work hard and grow together? Why not have the love and support, and the strength, and travel the road of success together? Because that's where happiness is: it's not in reaching the goal because when you get there, you're done, and then what? Happiness is on the way there. You need to enjoy every single day of your life that you spend on your way towards achieving things. Why don't you want to share these days with people who will have your interest at heart? It will be more fun that way. Even sex will be more easily accessible. Married people have more sex than single people. And then, there is the comfort you will get from the familiarity. That is if we don't want to mention anything about the fact that, when you are in a committed relationship, you will be avoiding the physical and emotional diseases that result from infidelity and promiscuity.

Why bring all that suffering onto ourselves? Why not be content with what we have now, while keeping our ambition for a better tomorrow? Why not cooperate and work hard together to achieve big things? Why antagonize the other sex? Why not take care of each other? Why not cook good meals for ourselves? They will always be cheaper than even fast food, and you will be eating gourmet food daily if you want. Have you noticed on "Cribs" on MTV that when they open their fridge, it is usually empty and has nothing appetizing in it at all whatsoever?

All these questions are simple and seem to have obvious answers, and yet, the sexes are not appreciating each other because there are very strong societal forces preventing that from happening. The women are trying to form families, and a lot of men aren't. Everybody ends up being in a compromised position and vulnerable to exploitation. What ends up taking place is "Divide and conquer." A lot of women have been propagating our species and raising children by themselves. The men need to understand what is happening at the conscious level and step up to the plate. A woman forms a home, but it is the man who forms a wholly stable family. Everybody needs to realize that one hand alone does not clap and that "there is strength in numbers."

RIGHT AND WRONG

Human beings know what's right and what's wrong because we are born with "measuring sticks" within us. Everybody with a normal nervous system and not under the influence of drugs or alcohol knows right from wrong. We mostly are aware whenever other people's good starts infringing on our good, or whenever our good starts infringing on other people's good. And if we are not aware, the people around us will be, and they'll make sure to let us know. They will create rules and regulations and the social systems needed to contain our behavior. We also have a natural inhibition to kill, except in self-defense. But even killing in self-defense is difficult to live with. That's why our veterans come back from war to years of suffering!

We know what's right and what's wrong, but people tune to the outside world a lot, especially when the outside noise is loud and constant. If people would tune internally, they would find the knowledge they need in there. So I'll tell you one thing only: tune in. Tune in because your brain knows what's right and wrong, and your body knows what's right for it, and what's not right for it also. When you tune in and understand, you will have better health.

The body has in it all the knowledge it needs to heal itself. There is also memory that restores it to its optimal health. A simple example: when you cut your skin, it is replaced with skin again. When you get a sinus infection, all your sinuses get inflamed and plugged up, and then they get restored to their original state. You break a bone, and when aligned, your body heals the fracture site with bone of the same shape as the original. All that the doctors do is remove an offensive thing like a disc compressing a nerve, or try to stop a destructive process, or repair a structure, and then the body does the actual healing by itself.

You want to lose weight? Bring back your memory from the time when you were skinny, and recall what you used to eat, and the way your body felt in space at that time. That will help you restore that memory.

Everybody is aware of the basic premise for the need to exercise and eat right. Your body knows what's best for it at each particular moment. You might be under the weather today, and don't feel like exercising...so don't. Then you heal, and you feel a surge of energy and the need to be more active physically... so do that. If you're craving something sweet now, then eat fruit. If you feel like a big steak, enjoy it. Just make sure that you don't overdo anything, and that you keep the balance. If you overeat today or indulge in decadent food, correct it tomorrow. Stay away from contaminated food, processed food, and from soft food and mild tastes.

Soft food does not require much chewing, and you end up swallowing a big quantity of it too fast, which does not give your body enough time to send the satiety signals to your brain when needed. So you end up overeating.

Mild tasting food does not satisfy the brain. Food taste is like musical notes. When you're eating mild tasting food, your brain entices you to eat more and more to be able to register it. When you eat food with a strong taste, your brain "gets it" in a short period of time, gets satisfied, and will not entice you to overeat. If your food does not have a strong taste, add herbs or spices to it—or lemon, vinegar or other condiments.

Therefore, dedicate time to preparing your own meals because that's the only way to make sure they include the right ingredients. It will be an activity a lot more entertaining and satisfying than watching cooking shows, and it will be cheaper and healthier than eating out.

Wake up and listen to your body, and your brain. People usually "wake up" and bring information from their subconscious to their conscious level when they need to make life-changing decisions, or in case of an emergency or pain (whether it is emotional or physical pain). Pain alerts the brain and wakes us up. Embrace it because it is necessary for survival and progress. "No pain, no gain!" It is the pain and suffering that results from lacking and wanting something that ends up giving people the oomph and endurance needed to achieve great things—whenever they decide to achieve those great things.

It is also your body's way of protecting itself. The people that are born with a genetic defect that causes them not to feel pain do not live beyond childhood. It's your body sending messages to your brain to tell you to do this or do that to protect it. Go see the doctor, for example, because you might have a treatable condition that might harm your health, or cost you your life if you don't.

Discomfort and pain are also meant to modulate your activities to keep your body in the healthiest shape possible. For example, we're not meant to stay in one position for too long. Even when we're sleeping, our body tosses and turns to keep its health optimal. But sometimes, certain circumstances force us to keep our bodies still, like when our attention gets captivated by a book, or the computer or watching TV. Keep in mind that you need to move every 15 to 20 minutes, and to stretch every once in a while. Even if you get up and walk around your chair then sit down, you would have done something beneficial to your body; and don't forget to incorporate stretching into your daily activities.

Stretching and using heat are beneficial because they improve the terminal circulation. That terminal circulation provides the nutrients to all of the body's living cells, the building blocks for repair, and cleans out waste. Improving its function and the health of your tissues will result in the improvement of your whole circulatory system and your general health. Stay close to nature in terms of what you put in your body and what you expose your body to, and keep everything in moderation. Our ancestors have lived close to nature, and we are the descendants of whoever has survived that laboratory experiment. Laboratory, yes! Nature is a giant laboratory in constant motion: what works stays, and what does not work vanishes.

Currently, we've been witnessing evolution in progress: the creation of the multi-taskers. Because of the explosive nature of the communication revolution, our world has been evolving around us at breakneck speeds. Everybody is trying to play catch-up. It is really hard to figure out how things will balance out and what the outcome will be. The best example is the phenomenon happening at educational institutions. It has become harder and harder to get the attention of the kids on one thing, because they are getting constantly distracted by their electronic gadgets and by electronic information. Too much is being thrown at them simultaneously, but I do trust that they will find within themselves all the answers. They just need to acquire knowledge, tune in, do their math correctly, and they'll find themselves on the right track.

EVOLUTION

One thing is certain though. The system has been set up in the way that every possibility that could happen, happens. What works at a certain time in an equation under some specific circumstances stays, and what doesn't work vanishes. Mutations are happening constantly. The viable ones survive, and the non-viable ones don't survive. For example, pesticides and insecticides fail to kill all of the pests and insects they are supposed to kill, because some of them already have a natural immunity to these chemicals. These immune pests and insects multiply, and generate more immune descendents. Similarly, in a colony of bacteria, some will have resistance to a certain antibiotic, and will be the only ones to survive treatment with it. They multiply and all their descendents will be resistant to it also. That is why there is no escaping it: when we are going to use antibiotics, if we kill all the bacteria that are sensitive, we are going to be left with the resistant ones only and no antibiotic to fight them with. On the other hand, if we don't kill all of the antibiotic sensitive bacteria, they might be able to keep the antibiotic resistant ones in check, and help us with our fight against them.

Those environmental stressors that modify the populations of organisms, insects and pests operate the same way on human beings. Some people used to get sick and die with tuberculosis (TB), and be taken care of by family members in the same household who do not get sick with TB. Some people get exposed to the new HIV virus and do not get AIDS from it, because they have a natural immunity to it. The same thing applies to people exposed to the herpes virus, the influenza virus, HPV, hepatitis or plague and so on and so forth. Natural selection is constantly happening around us.

Infection has been an essential part of evolution. It explains why things evolved so fast. Our mitochondria were a symbiotic parasitic infection into our cells—the result of which just happened to create the human being. We can witness the evolutionary process all the time, everywhere and in everything.

Finally, and to sum it all up, since God equals science, then the creationists and the evolutionists have been talking about one and the same thing, and the debate between them has actually been a disagreement over science using different rhetoric. Let's even out the rhetoric and then we will be able to understand each other. If God had come to us in the form of a human being as Jesus Christ in the past, then God has not been a human being since. So what is God? Nobody can debate that God is all encompassing and has all of the powers. God is all encompassing and is all of the powers. God is everything, and everything operates following scientific rules, including Intelligent Design.

No religion can debate that fact. The essence of all religions is actually the same and the difference between them is just rhetoric: allegories, metaphors and minutiae. In fact, the conservative people from one religion have some of the same exact beliefs as the conservative people from another religion, as if they all belonged to the same religion. For example, as the three abrahamic religions, Judaism, Christianity and Islam believe in a rewarding and punishing God, and in heaven and hell. Each one of them also believes that they are right and everybody else is wrong; that they will be going to heaven, and everybody else won't. They are more alike than the conservative and liberal from the same religion are. For instance, look at whom the conservative Muslim-Americans voted for in the year 2000: George W. Bush! Similarly, conservatives from other religions like Hindus and Sikhs vote for the conservative Christians also even though, the more conservative people are, the more xenophobic.

Therefore, followers of all religions fall on the same exact spectrum from the most conservative to the most liberal, and when you neutralize the rhetoric, what it boils down to is that there are different degrees of only two religions in the world: "Conservative" and "Liberal." The "Right" and the "Left." Coming closer together is ideal, because then the hands can clap!

Being on either extreme side of this spectrum is not good. The extreme Conservatives' bad actions have become obvious to everybody all over the world, and have not remained a mystery. Nobody can hide in his or her cloak anymore! While on the other hand, the extreme Liberals have inundated us enough with their filthy socially irresponsible messages and imagery! Enough! We've seen it all!

But as I have stated earlier, something good always comes out of the bad, because finally, the extreme-to-the-point-of-being-sickening-liberals and their supporters have put themselves in a corner. They have exposed all shocking things for the whole world to see—they've "put it all on the table." Actually, everything is out there in the digital realm, just a few keyboard clicks away from everybody's reach. We've seen the gay and recognized them as our brethren; we've seen the transvestites. We know people cheat and hurt each other. We realize that there is porn and promiscuity everywhere. In her video "Telephone," we've seen a murderous Lady Gaga's labia, thankyouverymuch! And then when you've seen one, you've seen them all: Now what? How are you going to top this?

Nothing can shock us anymore. What are you going to resort to next?

You've done some good for society, but on the other hand, you've done and continue to do some very bad deeds. You've deservedly exposed the extreme Conservatives for what they really are, but in the process of doing that; you've defamed all religion. You've sung the praises of irresponsibility, delinquency, antisocial behavior and indulgence in drugs and alcohol without any regard to how your actions are going to impact the public. Those ill societies you're fostering to fill your pockets with the greenbacks are the same ones your children and grandchildren are going to grow up in, and you forget that "what goes around comes around."

You don't care, right? It's all in the name of "free speech." But don't worry, we've got your game: If that's accurate, how come your free speech is heavily weighted with what's damaging and destructive as opposed to what's constructive and healing? Why don't you expose the bad consequences that result from the bad lifestyles you're promoting, like addictions, STDs and emotional diseases? Why? If you believe that exercising your free speech rights this way does not make you responsible for people's behavior, then shame on you for being irresponsible human beings! Because unfortunately, and to sell your wares, it is the minds of the younger clean-slated inexperienced generations that you are impacting the most, and I'm pretty sure you are aware of that.

Now it's time for you to get exposed. One thing I would tell you is this: If you had enough intelligence, you would have captured our attention using your brain, and you wouldn't have needed to resort to despicable filth to shock us into noticing you! So enough is enough: Hurry up and straighten your act out because the pendulum is starting to swing in the other direction.

A happy medium is where everybody needs to be, but that's not how things work in life. Rather, things swing like a pendulum between two extremes, and that's how they are kept in balance.

We can say that and surrender to the laws of nature the same way some women surrender when they have children out of wedlock. But is that all we can do? Is that our "destiny?" No it's not, because our world is thoughts that we should be able to control, and therefore, we do have a choice and our choices do make a difference.

THE ZERO

Here's a mind twister for you:
In the end, there is no beginning and there is no end.

I HEREBY DECLARE THE ZERO NULL AND VOID

For if the concept of the Zero is true, then the Zero
does not exist, and if the concept of the Zero is not true,
then the Zero does not exist. Therefore,
the Zero does not exist.
Therefore there is no beginning and there is no end.

THE END!